THE EMOTIVE THEORY OF ETHICS

D0718464

Philosophy

Editor
PROFESSOR H. J. PATON
MA, FBA, D.LITT, LL.D
Emeritus Professor of Moral Philosophy
in the University of Oxford

THE
EMOTIVE THEORY OF
ETHICS

J. O. Urmson

Fellow of Corpus Christi College, Oxford, and
University Lecturer in Philosophy

HUTCHINSON UNIVERSITY LIBRARY
LONDON

HUTCHINSON & CO (*Publishers*) LTD
178–202 Great Portland Street, London W1

London Melbourne Sydney
Auckland Bombay Toronto
Johannesburg New York

★

First published 1968

© J. O. Urmson 1968

*This book has been set in Fournier, printed in Great Britain
on Smooth Wove paper by Anchor Press, and
bound by Wm. Brendon, both of Tiptree, Essex*

09 087430 7 (cased)
09 087431 5 (paper)

CONTENTS

PREFACE

A Cambridge philosopher once said that, since the use of the definite article implies that there is only one thing to refer to, the use of the definite article in the expression 'The Oxford Movement' is an indication that Oxford has moved only once. Whatever truth there may be in this allegation, it would certainly be a mistake to suppose that there is but one emotive theory of ethics, because we speak of *the* emotive theory of ethics. There are in fact as many such theories as there are philosophers whose views can be so described. It would be impossible in a short book to discuss all these variations on the theme adequately. I have therefore chosen to make Stevenson's *Ethics and Language*, first published in 1944, my *terminus ad quem*, neglecting later and often more complicated versions except on a few sporadic points. Thus I do not discuss *The Logic of Moral Discourse* (1955) by Paul Edwards, though it is one of the most persuasive and certainly the liveliest statement of the emotive theory with which I am acquainted; I have neglected the modifications in his views made by Ayer in the preface to the second edition of his *Language, Truth and Logic*, and discussed his opinions only as presented in the original text of 1936; I have not taken into account Stevenson's restatement of his views in 'Meaning: descriptive and emotive' (*Philosophical Review*, 1947), in *Facts and Values* (1963) and in his contribution to *Ethics and Society* (Ed. De George, 1966). Therefore when in this book I speak of Ayer I refer to the author of the first edition of *Language, Truth and Logic*, and when I speak of Stevenson I refer to the author of the articles 'The emotive meaning of ethical terms' (1937) and 'Persuasive definitions' (1938), both published in *Mind*, and of the book *Ethics and Language*. I know that both have abandoned or would present in importantly different ways many of their views which I here criticise. These views are interesting, and it is they that I discuss, not their authors at a later period of their thought.

But discussion is not confined to these views of Ayer and Stevenson; some mention is made of earlier versions of the theory. These include the classical formulation in *The Meaning of Meaning* (1923) by Ogden and Richards; 'A suggestion about value' (*Analysis*, 1934) by W. H. F. Barnes; the views of Duncan Jones as reported by Broad in 'Is "goodness" the name of a simple non-natural quality?' (*Proceedings of the Aristotelian Society*, 1933–4); the account of emotive meaning in *Communication* (1939) by Karl Britton. It would not only be beyond my competence to present a fair survey of later literature; it would be of little interest to me to attempt it, and the philosophical points that I wish to make can be made most readily with reference to the earlier, simpler and less qualified versions of the theory.

While the discussions in this book are intended to be intelligible without reference to others, the reader who has already read the relevant portions of the sixth chapter of Ayer's *Language, Truth and Logic* and, say, the first ten chapters of Stevenson's *Ethics and Language* will be at an advantage. In any case this book is a discussion of the emotive theory which is not intended to be a substitute for the original presentations of the theory.

I have not been inhibited by the title of the book from giving my own opinions in some detail on various points on which I find the emotive theory inadequate. But I should not wish to regard these views as a version, even an improved one, of emotivism. I write as an admirer, but not an adherent, of the emotive theory of ethics.

Those potential readers who attended my course of lectures with the same title as this book, delivered at Oxford three or four times between 1960 and 1966, may like to be warned that the book is very similar in content to the lectures.   J.O.U.

I

PRELIMINARIES

No doubt the most important questions in the moral sphere are
those that are most concrete; it matters more that we should answer
correctly such questions as whether this or that, between which we
must choose, is better, or what we ought to do in the situation with
which we are faced, than that we should be clear on general moral
and philosophical issues. But if we raise such concrete practical
issues we often find it hard to find answers that are satisfactory even
for practical purposes, answers leaving us in no doubt how to act
and undisputed by others. Moreover, it is hard for us to see why
such answers as do recommend themselves to us are satisfactory; at
the best they may seem only to postpone a problem. We decide that
we ought not to pull the cat's tail because we ought not to be cruel
to animals, without thereby achieving any notable advance. Faced
with difficulties of this kind, difficulties so familiar to us all that it is
unnecessary to enlarge on them, men at all times have been con-
strained to raise the general question how in principle such particular practical problems are to be properly solved.

But as soon as we raise the question how a certain type of assertion, the moral, the mathematical or the aesthetic, for example, can
be reasonably arrived at or defended, it is clearly necessary to determine the general character of such assertions, to make it explicit
what sort of claims in what sorts of fields they make. Thus, to take
a platitudinous example from outside ethics, it is the beginning of
wisdom in determining how the assertions of pure mathematics are

to be rationally supported to see that at least they are not factual records of the way things are, so that it would be pointless to try to prove them by the collection of empirical evidence. If we want to know what sort of support a claim needs, we surely need to be clear what sort of a claim is being made.

We can make the point clearer to ourselves by briefly considering two analyses of one type of ethical judgement, both, I think, wildly unplausible, which have from time to time been proposed. According to these analyses it is not merely the case that right actions are in accord with the will of God or that right actions tend to promote the survival of the human species; the contention is that 'It is right to do action X' means exactly the same as, on the one view, 'Action X is in accordance with the will of God', or, on the other view, 'Action X tends to promote the survival of the human species'. It is irrelevant to discuss now the merits and demerits of either of these proposed analyses; the point is that if we could determine that one of these analyses was correct we should have completely determined how questions about the rightness of actions were to be decided. If the former analysis is correct, then obviously the way to decide how to act is to research into the revelations of God's will; and we shall thus be determining what is right, not indirectly by means of resorting to an infallible authority, but directly, since being right will be the same thing as being in accordance with God's will. If, on the other hand, we decided that rightness was the same thing as tending to promote the survival of the human species, then the way to determine how to act would be by an empirical, statistical investigation of the effect on human survival of different kinds of action; and, analogously to the former case, a tendency to promote the survival of the human race would not be merely a reliable sign of the rightness of an act, but the same thing as its rightness. Further, if we accept the theological analysis, but doubt the possibility of knowing the will of God, we shall have to be also moral sceptics; on the other analysis we may have to be temporary moral sceptics pending the development of a specialised branch of statistical sociology which will be the new science of ethics. Though we have considered, for illustrative purposes, two very implausible analytical theses, they none the less make clear the importance in ethical inquiry of the analysis of moral terms. We are continually and wearisomely admonished that to raise questions of moral analysis is to neglect substantive moral issues. It is certainly true that moral insight and philosophical insight are no substitutes for each other; but we may be led to seek the latter by a desire to achieve the former.

The point of this brief attempt to make clear the relevance of the analysis of ethical terms and utterances, apart, of course, from the intrinsic interest of such analysis to anybody with a suitable cast of mind, is that the emotive theory of ethics, our main concern in this book, is an analytical theory about the nature of ethical utterances, or at least claims to be such. It is reasonably clear that considerations similar to those adduced with regard to ethics arise also in the field of aesthetics and other areas in which evaluations are made. The analyses offered by the emotive theory were intended by most of its proponents to cover all cases of evaluation and not merely those found in moral contexts. 'The emotive theory of value judgements' might have been a better name for the view than 'The emotive theory of ethics'.

2

THE GROUNDS FOR EMOTIVISM

Before we start to examine the details of the emotive theory we should examine what have seemed to many philosophers (no doubt, erroneously) to be the only two other possibilities. If it be asked what is meant by saying of something that it is good, one possible answer seems to be that we thereby say something capable of empirical confirmation or overthrow; such an answer is called naturalistic.

If one asks what such a word as 'good' means it is manifestly implausible to answer that it stands for any fairly simple feature of things directly accessible to observation as do the words 'red', 'sweet' and 'loud', for example, and no naturalist would make such an answer. But it is not so manifestly unplausible to hold that it stands for some empirically determinable, though not directly observable, feature of things, just as it is a matter for empirical investigation, though not for direct observation, whether a certain chemical is or is not alkaline. Thus there is some plausibility in the view that 'good' means the same as 'satisfying desire'; if this view is correct, in its crudest form, then statements that things are good will require to be tested by empirical methods in a field of applied psychology closely allied to consumer research. It has also seemed plausible to some to say that 'good' means the same as 'approved by most people', in which case the test will again be in the field of empirical statistics. Many more naturalistic analyses have been suggested, some of them much more subtle than those given, but it would be out of place to consider such suggestions now.

Naturalism is, then, one possible type of ethical analysis. But many recent philosophers, including those who came to accept emotivism, have become convinced that there are general arguments which show that any form of naturalism is in principle erroneous. For our purposes the important fact is that these arguments were accepted by the emotivists and we need not enter the battle in support of them. It was G. E. Moore who first put forward the general arguments against naturalism. The main reason for rejecting it is simply that it is always clear, if we consider, that a thing having any natural features we care to think of may not be good, so that goodness cannot be identical with any of these natural features. Even if it were true, as it is not, that everything satisfying our desires was good, we could still envisage the possibility of something satisfying our desires and yet not being good; so 'good' cannot mean the same as 'satisfying our desires'.

This argument against naturalism seemed to Moore to be decisive also against any metaphysical or theological definition of 'good'. If, for example, we take the theological definition of 'good' as meaning the same as 'willed by God', it would follow from the definition that it would be self-contradictory to deny that what God wills is good. But the very falsity, impiety and blasphemy involved in denying that what God wills is good requires the view that 'good' means something different from 'willed by God'; to contradict oneself is futile rather than impious.

Thus naturalism had to be rejected, Moore thought. It seemed to him that the only view which could escape the naturalist fallacy was that 'good' named some absolutely simple characteristic; but, since it was clear that it did not name any simple sensible characteristic, since good things do not share some characteristic smell, taste, look, sound or feel never mentioned in empirical science, the only possible alternative seemed to him to be that 'good' was the name of a simple *non-natural* characteristic apprehended by the moral intelligence rather than by the senses. This view commended itself to many others as well as Moore in the earlier years of the twentieth century, especially in Britain. Ross, Prichard and the other intuitionists accepted it, as did even Russell for a time.

Thus the two existing possibilities with which the emotivists regarded themselves as faced were naturalism and non-naturalism—apparently an exhaustive dichotomy. But empirically minded philosophers could hardly accept Moore's solution. If there were technical reasons for rejecting the otherwise attractive naturalistic analysis of ethical terms, Moore's alternative, involving the acceptance of what amounted to *a priori* concepts, was impossible to accept on the most basic grounds. Moore himself understood very well what the situation was, and he well described it in *Philosophical Studies* (pp. 258–9): 'Many of those who hold strongly (as many do) that *all* kinds of value are "subjective" certainly object to the so-called "objective" view, not so much because it is *objective*, as because it is not *naturalistic* or *positivistic*. To a view which is at the same time both "naturalistic" or "positivistic" and also "objective", such as the Evolutionary view which I sketched just now [to the effect that 'good' means approximately the same as 'leading to survival'] they do not feel at all the same kind or degree of objection as to any so-called "objective" view. With regard to so-called "objective" views they are apt to feel not only that they are false, but that they involve a particularly poisonous kind of falsehood—the erection into a "metaphysical" entity of what is really susceptible of a simple naturalistic explanation. They feel that to hold such a view is not merely to make a mistake, but to make a superstitious mistake. They feel the same kind of contempt for those who hold it, which we are apt to feel towards those whom we regard as grossly superstitious, one which is felt by certain persons for what they call "metaphysics" '. Moore is undoubtedly right; in the language of the logical positivists we might say that these objective or non-natural characters are a kind of innate idea or *a priori* concept; consequently any sentence containing a word which is alleged to name a non-natural character must be unverifiable and therefore nonsensical. Naturalism was at the worst false, as Moore had no doubt shown; but non-naturalism was not a genuine alternative at all.

But subjectivism, the popularity of which Moore was explaining in the passage just quoted, was no third possibility for the philosopher who accepted Moore's attack on naturalism while rejecting his alternative. For a definition of 'good' is no less naturalistic, plainly, when couched in terms of goings on in the mind of the beholder than when couched in terms of any other transactions and therefore suffers from the same defects. So naturalistic definitions of value terms, it was held, were unacceptable on technical grounds, and this remained true whether the definition was in so-called 'objective' or 'subjective' terms; non-naturalism was on general epistemological grounds a non-starter. The dichotomy 'natural— non-natural' seemed to be exhaustive, yet 'good' seemed to have neither of these kinds of meaning. What were philosophers to say, once they had argued themselves into this position? The con-clusion that value terms do not have, or do not have only, a mean-ing of the kind envisaged, that they do not name any quality whether natural or, *per impossibile*, non-natural stares us in the face. We are familiar with this view nowadays, and we draw it from the premises, as a matter of formal logic, easily enough; it was drawn by I. A. Richards in 1923 and by a few other bold spirits in the years that followed, but it seemed at the time to be not an obvious conclusion but a bold new theory.

It should be noted that the considerations just adduced in support of the view that value words name no character or relation, whether natural or non-natural, are of a very general epistemological character and did not arise out of a careful and close reflection on the nature of value judgements. Thus considerations from epistemology and philosophy of language rather than from ethics were the original ground for the modern British-American emotive theory of value terms in its earliest formulations. That this general pre-sentation of the situation is correct can be confirmed by an examina-tion of the early history of emotivism.

The earliest statement of the emotive theory of value terms in the modern *British-American* tradition (as opposed to statements in such continental writers as Haegerstroem which became known to English-speaking philosophers only comparatively late and had no early influence) was, so far as I know, that given by I. A. Richards in a general linguistic and epistemological work, *The*

Meaning of Meaning, written in conjunction with C. K. Ogden and published in 1923. Some of their most important remarks are conveniently quoted, facing the Preface, in Stevenson's *Ethics and Language* (though he does not give the reference, which is to page 125 of the second edition). We need quote only the historic sentence: 'The peculiar ethical use of "good" is, we suggest, a purely emotive use.' The general context makes clear, as the title of the book implies, that this remark is made in the context of a general theory of meaning.

The next reference to the emotivist analysis that I have noticed is, once again, in a non-ethical work; it is in Susan Stebbing's *A Modern Introduction to Logic* (1930), a general logic which makes no pretence to take a special interest in value theory. There Stebbing says: 'Many statements are made, however, not for the sake of conveying information, but in order to arouse in the hearer a certain response, to create in him a certain state of mind. . . . To mark the distinction Mr I. A. Richards has suggested the convenient terminology "the scientific use of language" and "the emotive use of language". . . When [language] is used in order to arouse an emotional attitude in the hearer, to influence him in any way other than by that of giving him information, then its use is *emotive*.' (op. cit., pp. 16–19). Like Richards, speaking in the context of a discussion of meaning in general, Stebbing does not pursue the topic further.

The first time, so far as I can ascertain, that the emotive theory was advocated in print in a specifically ethical context was March 1934, when it was stated by W. H. F. Barnes in his brief 'A suggestion about value', published in *Analysis;* this was apparently a fragment of a paper on Hartmann's *Ethics* read to the Jowett Society at Oxford. It is impossible to determine from this brief extract what Barnes's main theme was, but having begun by saying that 'value judgements in their origin are not strictly judgements at all. They are exclamations expressive of approval', much of the three short paragraphs is devoted to distinguishing this expressive view from subjectivism and discussing its relation to naturalism and non-naturalism; so apparently the problem is once again how to escape from that dichotomy. An interesting feature of Barnes's view is that he says that value judgements in their origin are not judgements at all, but exclamations of approval, and goes on to say that they 'will only express meaning in so far as the society in which they are used is agreed on what things it approves. And then "good" and "value" will be terms that have meaning only by referring to the actual nature of the thing.' Thus Barnes anticipates in a rudimentary way both the first and the second patterns of analysis offered by Stevenson, but does not, strictly, advocate an emotive theory of meaning; he recognised only 'descriptive' or 'cognitive' meaning and regards the expression of approval as the pre-meaningful origin. Here we have not the emotive theory of the meaning of ethical terms, but the emotive theory in the making.

We find the full-fledged emotive theory stated for the first time in an ethical context in June 1934, when it was outlined, with an attribution to A. S. Duncan Jones, by Broad in an article entitled 'Is "goodness" the name of a simple non-natural quality?' The article appeared in the *Proceedings of the Aristotelian Society*, 1933–4, the relevant pages being 250–4. Here, once again, the discussion arises out of the epistemological problem of definition rather than from a close examination of ethical discourse, and the chief merit that Duncan Jones is quoted as claiming for his theory is that 'it explains why all attempts to define ethical words in purely non-ethical terms seem unsatisfactory'. Incidentally, we find in Broad's article the first instance of a once popular version of the emotive theory when he offers, non-committally, as an analysis of a statement that a certain act was good: 'That's an act of self-sacrifice. Hurrah!' From this, and parallel examples in which 'Boo!' takes the place of 'bad', arose the name 'the boo-hurrah theory of ethics' which the emotive theory was often given in the 1930s.

We find an essentially similar background to the emotive theory if we examine the contribution of the logical positivists. Wittgenstein, in his *Tractatus Logico-Philosophicus*, most notably in the paragraphs numbered 6.4 to 6.421, had denied meaning to ethical propositions and called them nonsensical on the ground that they were neither significant like empirical truth-functions nor empty of sense, though well formed, like the necessary truths of logic. In line with this the logical positivists of the Vienna Circle had declared ethical judgements to be nonsense. Once again, this judgement was not made on the merits of the case, and after careful attention to the character of ethical discourse; ethical discourse was nonsensical as being neither empirical nor tautological. Thus Carnap, on page 26 of his *Philosophy and Logical Syntax*, published in 1935, revealingly says that value judgements have 'no theoretical sense. Therefore we assign them to metaphysics.' So what the logical positivists had to say about ethics (with a few exceptions, such as Schlick in his *Fragen der Ethik*) applied to ethics merely as being a sub-branch of metaphysics, in the esoteric sense in which they used that word. But there was a general formula in use among the logical positivists for explaining the prevalence and attractiveness of the many kinds of metaphysical nonsense that they had diagnosed—moral talk, religious and theological talk, aesthetic talk, and so on. It was allowed that all these ways of talking were attractive because they were one and all ways of expressing our emotions; it was very common to say that metaphysics (a word used dyslogistically to cover all the newly recognised varieties of nonsense) was a way of expressing emotion similar to poetry. So, I repeat, we find the logical positivists assigning the role of expression of emotion to ethical discourse, on the very general ground that it was a variety of metaphysical nonsense, the whole phenomenon being inexplicable unless it was supposed that the utterance of such nonsense gave some sort of emotional relief or satisfaction.

We have now, perhaps, sufficiently established that the original ground for the proposal of the emotive theory was the need to find some way out from the unacceptable dichotomy of naturalism and non-naturalism. It is against this background that the well-known and influential 'critique of ethics' in Ayer's *Language, Truth and Logic*, published in 1936, has to be examined. Chapter VI of that book revealingly begins as follows: 'There is still one objection to be met before we can claim to have justified our view that all synthetic propositions are empirical hypotheses.' This objection is that value judgements are synthetic, but not empirical, since ethical terms cannot be naturalistically analysed. 'In face of this objection, it is our business to give an account of "judgements of value".' While Ayer immediately recognises that this account must be satisfactory in itself, and while he gives a very lively account of the matter which makes it still the best reading of all short accounts of the emotivist thesis, it is once again the general epistemological problem, already so familiar, that is in the forefront of the discussion. It is striking, as one reads through the text, that, while Ayer takes great pains to show that the view that ethical utterances express and evoke emotion is not vulnerable to certain stock objections brought against subjectivist and other ethical theories, he at no stage tries very hard to show that his view best explains our actual procedures in moral thinking and discussion, to show positively that it is a happy account of the phenomena. This, given the scope of the book, is not to be taken as adverse criticism.

So the emotive theory of ethics has its origin in epistemological despair. There is no account of the meaning of ethical utterances hitherto proposed which is epistemologically acceptable, since naturalism is unfortunately false and non-naturalism abhorrent. If this were all there was to say about emotivism it could hardly claim any sustained interest. But in fact there are more positive reasons for accepting the emotive theory than these general epistemological considerations, and to these we can now turn.

Just as the seeds of the general epistemological argument can be found, retrospectively, in Hume, so can the essentials of this further ground for emotivism. In the section of the Second Book of the *Treatise of Human Nature* entitled 'Of the influencing motives of the will', Hume had declared that reason was, and ought to be, the servant of the passions. Only a passion could directly move us to action, for reason was capable only of informing us of matters of fact and their inferential relationships. But in face of a mere matter of fact we could always without logical fault maintain any attitude whatsoever. Let us suppose that by observation and inductive reasoning I discover that a certain drinking-glass contains poison; that fact, on its own, is powerless to move me to drink, or to refrain from drinking, or to give it to another to drink, or to restrain another from drinking. Reason, in informing me of this fact, can be only a servant of some desire to save my life or that of another, to murder or to commit suicide. Now what Hume called a matter of fact is what, according to the way of speaking of the period now under review, is the content of a scientific, or descriptive, or cognitive use of language. Further, both the naturalistic and the non-naturalistic analyses of ethical terms make out value judgements to be scientific, cognitive, or descriptive; they treat value judgements as reporting a mere matter of fact. This is no less the case if, in the case of non-naturalism, the fact must be regarded as non-natural, as belonging to metaphysical rather than to natural science.

Now, if Hume is right, we must accept that it is always possible to take any attitude whatsoever, without irrationality, in the face of any set of mere matters of fact. We have seen also that if we accept either naturalism or non-naturalism we are committed to the view that value judgements are mere statements of matters of fact. It follows logically that on either a naturalistic or a non-naturalistic interpretation of value judgements we can combine any attitude whatsoever with any value judgement without irrationality. But it has seemed obvious to many (including naturalists and non-naturalists) that this is not true. To say that something is bad or wrong is to commit oneself to an attitude and to give what, if not disputed, is an utterly sufficient reason for avoiding that thing; similarly we have already embraced an attitude if we say that something is right or good, and we have given a good reason for its pursuit. If a drink is poisonous it is irrational to take it only if you have the will to live; without the will to live one can rationally say that the drink is poisonous but there is no reason for not drinking it. But one cannot rationally say that it would be wrong to take the drink but that there is no reason for not drinking it. If we accept both this and the previous argumentation we can conclude only that neither naturalism nor non-naturalism does justice to the nature of value judgements; it is their failure to account for the distinctive features of value judgements, and the role they play in our life and thought, that is now invoked, rather than any general epistemological contentions about the conditions of significant discourse.

So we now have a new and quite different ground for rejecting both naturalism and non-naturalism. We no longer regretfully dismiss naturalism because (bother it!), whenever we suggest that 'good' may be defined as equivalent to the naturalistic description 'XYZ' Moore intervenes and points out that he can significantly doubt whether all XYZ things are good. We now have a positive reason, connected with the observed powers of ethical judgements, to look for another sort of analysis that will explain these powers. If we find that the emotive theory satisfies this requirement, we shall have better reason for accepting the emotive theory than that we cannot think what ethical judgements might do except express emotions if they do not state facts. We must now have a look at the historical material to find out whether the emotive theorists were in fact influenced by this line of argument, and whether they claimed that the emotive analysis could explain the special feature of value judgements to which we have just directed attention.

In the writers whom we have so far considered there is certainly nothing approaching a full-scale statement of this argument. The nearest approach to anything more than the view that in making ethical judgements we are venting our emotions and thus letting off steam is to be found in such remarks of Ayer as: 'It is worth mentioning that ethical terms do not serve only to express feeling. They are calculated also to arouse feeling, and so to stimulate action.' We need not suppose that they were all unsympathetic to, or ignorant of, the line of argument that we are now considering. The truth is that they were all exclusively interested in epistemological questions of a very general character and would have regarded any detailed discussion of ethical matters for their own sake as being, in the context, a mere digression. Moral philosophy was, as such, unpopular among empiricists at this period.

The first occasion known to me on which anything like the positive argument for emotivism now under consideration was deployed in print was in the paper which also seems to me to be the first written by any emotivist with a primary interest in morality itself. This paper is C. L. Stevenson's 'The emotive meaning of ethical terms', which appeared in *Mind* in 1937. It is no belittlement of Stevenson's other merits to say that his most important, historically, is that he was the first emotivist of all to take ethics seriously, for its own sake, in print. It would be idle to summarise this economically written article, which all should read; it is sufficient for our purposes at present to draw attention to his use in this article of the line of argument at present under consideration.

In the first section of this paper Stevenson argues that any adequate analysis of the term 'good' must fulfil three requirements. The first is that it should make it possible for us to disagree on questions of goodness, since in fact we do so; the third requirement is that the analysis should not make it a mere question of empirical fact whether something is good, which is open to anti-naturalistic objections. But there is a second requirement sandwiched between these two; it is that 'goodness must have, so to speak, a magnetism. A person who recognises X to be "good" must *ipso facto* acquire a stronger tendency to act in its favour than he otherwise would have had.' In the second part of the paper Stevenson continues: 'Traditional interest theories hold that ethical statements are *descriptive* of the existing state of interests—that they simply *give information* about interests. (. . . It is this emphasis on description, on information, which leads to their incomplete relevance. Doubtless there is always *some* element of description in ethical judgements, but this is by no means all. Their major use is not to indicate facts, but to *create an influence*. Instead of merely describing people's interests, they *change* or *intensify* them. They recommend an interest in an object, rather than state that the interest already exists.)' In the third part of his paper Stevenson calls this use of language one among a number of dynamic uses of words. After further argument and explanation he continues: 'There will be a kind of meaning, however, . . . which has an intimate relation to dynamic usage. I refer to "emotive" meaning (in a sense roughly like that employed by Ogden and Richards). The emotive meaning of a word is a tendency of a word, arising through the history of its usage, to produce (result from) *affective* responses in people'.

Stevenson goes on to explain how the emotive meaning of words can result in a dynamic use of language. Finally he explains how 'good' and other value words have emotive meaning and can thus contribute to a dynamic use of language and shows how his view thus meets the three requirements from which he started.

We shall have occasion later to criticise the details of Stevenson's views; enough has now been said to show that he does give a version of the argument under consideration. Ethical utterances, he holds, are to be interpreted according to the emotive theory of the meaning of ethical terms not only because of the technical difficulties raised against the rival descriptive theories but because ethical judgements are seen to be dynamic; the emotive theory gives a positive explanation how ethical judgements can be what Hume called 'influencing motives of the will'. At last we have some positive ground for ascribing an emotive meaning to value judgements.

3

EMOTIVE MEANING

We have now examined two of the routes by which philosophers were led to the position that there was a class of words whose important feature was the possession of emotive meaning, either as opposed to, or in addition to, scientific, cognitive, or descriptive meaning. This class included notably all value terms, among them those of ethical discourse. On the one hand they were led to this view by a theory of meaning which had no use for terms naming non-natural qualities and relations, combined with a recognition that it was implausible to give naturalistic definitions of evaluative terms. We have also observed that those who were particularly influenced by these general epistemological considerations were often merely consigning ethical utterances to the limbo of nonsense—they were allowed emotive expression in the same way that 'the nothing nothings' was conceded an emotional aura. On the other hand, some philosophers with a serious interest in ethics, such as Stevenson, were led to develop the emotive theory also because it seemed to recognise in ethical judgements a dynamic character absent from the static records of history and hypotheses of science.

What then is it for an expression to have emotive meaning? The term 'emotive meaning' is technical, and does not bear its meaning on its face to be read by any attentive observer. We must look first at some of the earlier explanations of the term in order to understand its later history.

(1) 'The emotive use of words is a more simple matter [*sc.* than the symbolic use], it is the use of words to express or excite feelings and attitudes.' (Ogden and Richards, *The Meaning of Meaning*, p. 149.) Ogden and Richards also speak of emotive expressions as evoking attitudes and inciting to action.

(2) '[A sentence] may be in part the expression of an emotion which the speaker is feeling. . . . Again, a sentence may be used partly to evoke a certain kind of emotion in the hearer.' (Broad, 'Is "goodness" the name of a simple non-natural quality?', in *Proceedings of the Aristotelian Society*, 1933–4.)

(3) (a) '[By calling an action wrong] I am simply evincing my moral disapproval of it. . . . I am merely expressing certain moral sentiments.' (Ayer, *Language, Truth and Logic*, 107.)

(b) 'In every case in which one would commonly be said to be making an ethical judgement the function of the relevant ethical word is purely "emotive". It is used to express feeling about certain objects.' (ibid., p. 108.)

(c) '[Ethical terms] are calculated also to arouse feeling, and so to stimulate action.' (ibid., p. 108.)

(d) 'We hold that ethical terms are expressions and excitants of feeling.' (ibid., pp. 109–10.)

(4) 'The emotive meaning of a word is a tendency of a word, arising through the history of its usage, to produce (result from) *affective* responses in people. It is the immediate aura of feeling which hovers about a word.' (Stevenson, 'The emotive meaning of ethical terms', *Mind*, 1937, p. 23.)

(5) 'The emotive meaning of a sign is an emotional response which a sign regularly produces in any normal listener who is familiar with its use.' (Karl Britton, *Communication*, 1939, p. 13.)

We may well pause to collect together this wealth of information. We may conveniently summarise it as follows: when an expression has emotive meaning it

expresses (1, 2, 3a, 3b, 3d)   emotion (2), feelings (1, 3b, 3d), attitudes (1), moral sentiments (3a).

excites (1, 3d)	feelings (1, 3d), attitudes (1).
incites to (1)	action (1).
evokes (1, 2)	attitudes (1), emotion (2).
evinces (3a)	moral disapproval (3a).
arouses (3c)	feeling (3c).
produces (4, 5)	affective response (4), emotional response (5).
results from (4)	affective response (4).
stimulates (3c)	action (3c).

A few comments follow; first on the objects that follow these various verbs.

(1) Action is mentioned, but only incidentally; Ogden and Richards speak of 'perhaps invoking similar attitudes in other persons or inciting them to actions' while discussing the meaning of 'this is good', but do not mention action in their formal account of emotive meaning; Ayer also merely notes once in passing that ethical terms are calculated to stimulate action. Yet the uninitiated might well suppose that morality was more concerned with our actions than with our emotions.

(2) Attitudes are mentioned only by Ogden and Richards in contexts which are explicative of the expression 'emotive meaning'; the word 'attitude' barely occurs in the Stevenson article, though he used it often in later writings. Ogden and Richards couple attitudes with feelings without any attempt to differentiate them. We shall have to inquire later whether the distinction between attitude and emotion is in fact so negligible.

(3) As one would expect from the name 'emotive meaning', the bulk of the objects suggested are some sort of feeling or emotion. When Stevenson speaks of an *affective* response, the italics being his, the aim is presumably to make it clear that the primary response at least is neither cognitive nor conative. Action is once again pushed into the background. We shall see that in later writings Stevenson and his allies continue to speak in terms of feelings and emotions when the context cries out for them to be talking about

something much more practical, such as action and attitude. The explanation is, it seems, that they started off with this conception of purely affective response which we have been noticing, and hardly saw how severely they were straining the expression 'emotive' in their later writings, so that they could speak as though they continued to use the conception of emotive meaning in its pristine form. At least they failed explicitly to repudiate this early version.

Let us now turn to examine the verbs that go with these objects. They fall, at first sight and on one principle of classification, into two groups. First, one group of verbs has to do with the state of the person using the expressions with emotive meaning; it includes *expresses*, *evinces*, and *results from*. The other group of verbs is concerned with the possible state of persons who hear the expressions; it includes *excite*, *incite to*, *evoke*, *arouse*, *produce*, *stimulate*. This grouping is of course the one which the philosophers under consideration wished to bring out. But can we regard the words in each of these groups as near synonyms between which it is hard, and perhaps pointless, to make a final choice? The fact that Ayer, for example, used more than one word from each group without apparently feeling any call to explain or defend this procedure suggests that he at least regarded them as little more than stylistic variants.

But, in the terminology made familiar by J. L. Austin in his *How to Do Things with Words*, in each group we find examples both of verbs naming an illocutionary force and of verbs naming a perlocutionary effect. Roughly, the illocutionary force of an utterance is what one is doing *in* issuing the utterance, whereas the perlocutionary effect is what one brings about *by* issuing the utterance. Thus, if I say 'Give it to me', the utterance may have, depending on context, intonation and the like, the illucutionary force of requesting, ordering or advising; for *in* saying 'Give it to me' I may be requesting, ordering or advising someone to hand it over. The perlocutionary effect may be that the person addressed gives it to me, or is offended, or promises to consider the matter; for *by* saying 'Give it to me' I may bring about one or other of these effects. Questions about illocutionary force are thus questions about how an utterance is to be taken—as an order, as a request or as advice, for example. Questions about perlocutionary effect are questions about the results of the issuing of the utterance.

In the light of this distinction we may consider first the list *excite, incite to, evoke, arouse, produce, stimulate.* We may suppose that, at the barricades, I shout 'A bas les aristos'. It may well be, the context being suitable, that in shouting 'A bas les aristos' I am inciting the bystanders to rebellion; incitement is an example of the possible illocutionary force of an utterance. It may also turn out that by shouting 'A bas les aristos' I excite or stimulate or arouse the people to rebellion, or produce a rebellion; equally, though trying to excite, stimulate or arouse the people to rebellion, I may, by shouting this coarse slogan, in fact arouse, produce or stimulate sympathy with the aristocrats clean contrary to my intention; here we have examples of intended and unintended perlocutionary consequences of an utterance. To put the point more shortly, to shout 'A bas les aristos' is a form that incitement to rebellion might take, whereas it can be only a fallible means towards exciting, producing, stimulating or arousing a revolt, and may well produce the direct opposite. But however injudicious in timing and placing, however disastrous in its consequences, it could not possibly count as inciting to sympathy with the aristocrats even if such sympathy was excited. Though it is not so clear as in the case of the other verbs, it seems that 'evoke' also names a perlocutionary rather than an illocutionary force. We should say 'He tried to evoke a mood of serenity but failed' rather than 'He evoked a mood of serenity, but unsuccessfully'; evocation of the mood did not consist in what he said but was an attempted product of it.

Now it seems clear that convention can determine what illocutionary force an utterance has in a given context, and even clearer that convention cannot assign to any expression a perlocutionary force, which has to be discovered empirically. Thus convention can determine that in the context my cry of 'A bas les aristos' is incitement to rebellion, but no convention can determine that this cry shall excite the people to rebellion. It is obviously true that only because of certain conventions of meaning in French could there be any hope of exciting the people to rebellion by shouting 'A bas les aristos', but this does not alter the fact that it is by convention an incitement to, but is not by convention a cause of, rebellion.

The application of these considerations to the question of the nature of emotive meaning is simple and, no doubt, already obvious. In so far as certain evaluative terms, when uttered, evoke, produce, stimulate or arouse any feeling, emotion, attitude or action this is simply a fact of empirical sociology, not a conceptual truth discoverable by philosophical analysis; these terms cannot achieve these effects by anything remotely resembling conventions of language or meaning rules, and if this is all that there is to say about them it is absurd to talk about emotive meaning. On the other hand, whether or not an utterance constitutes an incitement to an attitude or an action is a non-empirical, conventional issue, depending in part, at least, on the meaning of what is uttered; the verb 'incite' is therefore more appropriate than any of the others, with the possible exception of 'evoke', to occur in an analysis of meaning, so that it is strange that it occurs comparatively rarely in the literature.

One extended illustration of the importance of this point may not be an unnecessary extravagance. In a symposium in the Supplementary Volume of the *Proceedings of the Aristotelian Society* of 1948, entitled 'The emotive theory of ethics', Mr Richard Robinson tried to illustrate what he meant by saying that a word had independent emotive meaning as follows: 'Perhaps you will agree that the following list contains at least one pair of words that name the same thing but arouse different emotions towards it:

> to ape—to imitate
> nigger—negro
> etc., etc.'

In the course of a rightly puzzled discussion of this Mr Cross said: 'The word "nigger", however, does not function in the way of arousing *in me* a different emotion towards the object from that which the word "negro" does. So far as emotions are concerned, the only change that perhaps occurs is that I feel an emotion of dislike for the man who uses the word "nigger" instead of the word "negro".' But clearly Cross in no way failed to understand the word 'nigger'—as he goes on to say, he can infer that the speaker dislikes the object named; that the word fails to arouse a similar emotion of dislike in Cross is in no way a breakdown in communication. It follows that when Robinson said that 'emotive meaning is the power of a word to express and arouse feeling' he was either choosing the wrong word when he used the perlocutionary 'arouse' or he must have been using the word 'meaning' in a very extended sense. It would have been at least more plausible to say that the use of the word 'nigger' was an incitement to dislike of the object named. A convention of a linguistic kind can determine that an utterance is an expression of feeling, or an incitement to feeling, but not that it should arouse a feeling. The meaning of a word can hardly be a function of the suggestibility of its auditors.

We may now turn to the three verbs which have to do with the affective state of the user of the word in question; these were *express*, *evince* and *result from*. Once again it is clear that whether my uttering a certain word results from my having a certain emotion or feeling or attitude is not a question of meaning, but is rather psychological or biographical; the answer to the question may reflect favourably or unfavourably, on my sincerity, but hardly on my linguistic capacity. Perhaps I may have been conditioned to utter the word in question only when I have a certain feeling, but that makes no relevant difference that I can see; I have been more or less successfully conditioned to look interested when I am bored, but by looking interested I do not mean that I am bored.

But *express* is a more promising candidate. There is nothing odd in saying that a certain utterance was the expression of a feeling or attitude; expression of feeling may be an illocutionary force. Moreover whether certain words do express a certain feeling may, at least sometimes, depend in part on linguistic convention. What, then, can count as the expression of a feeling, attitude or emotion?

It is not at all clear what the limits to the use of the word 'express' are. The following examples seem to be clearly within them:

(a) Saying 'Father, I have sinned against heaven and in thy sight, and am no more worthy to be called thy son' counts as an expression of contrition.

(b) Squeezing somebody's hand can count in suitable circumstances as an expression either of affection or of sympathy.

(c) Saying 'I am very angry' counts as an expression of anger.

(d) Saying 'I approve of that' counts as an expression of approval.

The following cases seem to be clearly outside the limits:

(x) An involuntary groan is not an expression of agony.

(y) Unforced tears are not an expression of sorrow.

(z) Saying 'He approves of that' is not an expression of approval.

But there are intermediate cases that are difficult. I should be inclined to call dancing for joy an expression of joy even if it was not designed to let the joy be known; but if I gave somebody a present and he did nothing like saying 'I like this enormously', though he obviously gloated over it, I should be inclined to say that he had failed to express his manifest pleasure. It seems, however, that for something to count as an expression of a feeling it must be intentional; this, perhaps distinguishes the expression of a feeling from other manifestations of it. One may unintentionally betray one's feelings, but can one express them unintentionally?

However, we do not perhaps need to decide now the more tricky questions that arise about expression. It is at least abundantly clear that some utterances can be, by convention, expressions (sincere or deceitful) of a feeling, and that, therefore, utterances containing value words may have a meaning which consists in the expression of a feeling, so far as the use of 'express' in correct English goes. It is clear also that 'express' is like 'incite' rather than like 'excite' in the respects already noted. Something may be an expression of gratitude however unnoticed it may pass; in doing it I express my gratitude, rather than try to express my gratitude by doing it.

Let us, then, take it that 'express' is a better word to use than the alternatives that we have noticed in giving an account of emotive meaning. But still, if the project is to distinguish evaluative from non-evaluative ('scientific' or 'cognitive') expressions, to say that an expression has emotive meaning if it expresses the speaker's emotion is very inadequate. For, as we have already noticed, 'I am very angry' may certainly be an expression of anger, yet no emotive theorist would have wished to count it as a value judgement, or any of the words it contains as value terms. Again, the utterance 'I shall never forget this' may well in suitable circumstances express an emotion of gratitude felt by the speaker, but it would not have been counted as a value judgement. Indeed, a wide variety of utterances may, in suitable contexts, be expressions of emotion, so that this feature cannot on its own mark off the kind of utterance which emotive theorists had in mind. Ayer, for one, did not wholly neglect this point. Having noted that 'I am bored' may be at once an assertion and an expression of boredom, he says that the characteristic which he wishes to ascribe to ethical statements is that they 'are expressions . . . of feeling which do not necessarily involve any assertion' (*Language, Truth and Logic*, 2nd ed., p. 109). But this is hardly precise enough to incorporate into a definition.

The difficulties that arise here are acute and we shall have to return to them towards the end of this book. The problem is whether illocutionary force, any more than perlocutionary force, can be used to explain the alleged special kind of meaning possessed by value terms. But a reasonably clear account, for our present purposes, of what the emotivists had in mind might run somewhat as follows. A word, or expression, let us say, has emotive meaning if it serves by linguistic convention to express some emotion; it has pure emotive meaning if it has no other conventional force except to express emotion. Thus 'I shall never forget this' has not got emotive meaning because it expresses gratitude, when it does, only in virtue of a special non-linguistic context, not because of conventions governing any expression which it contains; in another extra-linguistic context it might express anger, for example, or no emotion at all. 'He is a nigger' may be said to have emotive meaning since (nowadays in most English-speaking societies) the use of the word 'nigger', instead of 'negro', involves by linguistic convention the expression of somewhat contemptuous superiority. It is a matter of meaning since an English speaker who did not realise this would have a defective command of the language. But the word 'nigger' has not pure emotive meaning, since by convention its use involves more than the expression of contempt. On the other hand, the exclamation spelt 'pshaw' and defined in one dictionary as expressing impatience, contempt and the like presumably has pure emotive meaning; it expresses impatient contempt by linguistic convention, so that it would be an abuse of language to use it for any quite different purpose, and it has this linguistic role exclusively. Opinion among the emotivists was divided about whether a word like 'good' had pure emotive meaning; according to Ayer, for example, it had; according to Stevenson it had not.

Finally, 'evince' occurs on our list, though it was in less frequent use. It is given a definition in one dictionary which I have consulted as 'show that one has (a quality, trait, etc.)'. If we accept this, and emphasise 'show' in a precise sense in which we cannot substitute for it the non-illocutionary 'betray', it does seem that 'evince' is a near-synonym of 'express'; we could substitute it in the examples (a), (b) and (c) above to form permissible sentences, and in (x), (y) and (z) to form illegitimate sentences, as in the case of 'express', and without notable change of meaning in the permissible cases.

Our survey of the terms used in the explanations of the notion of emotive meaning which we had collected is complete, and it is now time to draw the threads together, so far as we have gone. We found that a number of different verbs were used by emotive theorists to indicate the relation of expressions with emotive meaning to the emotions, feelings or attitudes of the speaker and his hearers. Of those commonly used to indicate the relation of the expression with emotive meaning to the speaker's emotion, feeling or attitude, we found that 'express' and 'evince' were near-syno-

B

nyms and could both with some plausibility be used to elucidate meaning, whereas 'result from' clearly indicates a mere causal relation which only very perverse supporters of a causal theory of meaning could regard as being in any way explicative of meaning. Of the verbs used to indicate the relation of the emotive expression to the hearer's emotion, feeling or attitude, we found that all (*excite*, *evoke*, *arouse*, *produce* and *stimulate*) save one (*incite*) suffered from the same unsatisfactory features as *result from;* meaning is a conventional matter, while none of these verbs indicate a relation in any way conventional. *Incite* is in its general character, if not in precise shade of meaning, appropriate to the same degree as is *express;* but we noticed that it was used only casually, only by Ogden and Richards, and with action rather than emotion or feeling as its object. Though we are being introduced to an emotive theory, there is no appropriate verb used with regard to hearer's emotions.

We have here come face to face with a point of great importance. Ogden and Richards spoke good English, and it is no accident that they made action rather than emotion the possible object of incitement. It would be very quaint to speak of inciting people to feel certain emotions. To put it crudely, we have to be incited to things which it is within our power to choose or reject, as we can choose or reject a course of action; but feelings and emotions, while they can no doubt be successfully cultivated over a period of time, can hardly be chosen as can actions and, perhaps, attitudes. We may choose to cultivate an emotion, but this is to choose a course of action. Thus, of those put forward to treat of the hearer's reactions, the only word that has the right general character to explain meaning seems inappropriate if the reactions in question are feelings and emotions. This is, to put it mildly, unfortunate when we are trying to explain what is called emotive meaning.

But if 'incite' is the right sort of verb in general logical character, if something can be an incitement by linguistic convention, can we think of another verb which would have the same general suitability but could admit feelings and emotions as the reactions to be connected conventionally with the expression with emotive meaning?

One might try 'recommend'; but, though I might recommend you to cultivate a certain emotion, can I recommend you to feel an emotion any more than I can incite you to do so? Once again, it seems to be actions rather than emotions that can be recommended. The difficulty is that while it is easy and appropriate enough for there to be conventional methods for a speaker to express an emotion which he has, or feigns to have, and while it is equally easy to have a conventional linguistic description or prediction of a hearer's emotions, it is hard indeed to see by what linguistic convention an expression could be conventionally linked to an emotion that one thinks it would be nice or desirable for the hearer to experience. I can, of course, express or describe an emotion which I think it would be desirable for you to feel, but that is clearly not what is required. We might try making it a linguistic convention that the word 'floreat' should be used only in conjunction with the name of an emotion, and that it should be a linguistic convention that one exclaimed 'Floreat anger' only when one wished to indicate the desirability of the emotion of anger in one's hearer; we might then claim that some similar convention exists already in the case of words with emotive meaning. But the trouble now is that 'Floreat anger' is manifestly rather an expression of my attitude or feeling about another's feeling angry than one which stands in a meaning relation to the anger of others.

I see no way out of this difficulty for those who wish to give a strictly emotive theory of meaning. There are in fact two possible lines open to anyone who wishes to investigate the relations holding between evaluative utterances and the states, actual and potential, of hearers of such utterances. First, we may take a purely empirical line; we may, for example, hold that evaluative language is a rhetorical device to produce or excite or stimulate or arouse emotions and feelings. We can then, if we wish, offer some psychological or sociological or rhetorical explanation of why it produces the effects that it does. But if we take this sort of line we should abandon all pretence to have thereby given any account of the logical character of evaluation language. Otherwise we can take the line that to use evaluative language is by linguistic convention to incite or recommend (or something similar) people to perform certain actions or adopt certain attitudes, rather than to have certain feelings or emotions. This will now be some account, though perhaps a false one, of the meaning of evaluative terms. For example, it might be held that to say of something that it was good was as much to incite people to act and hold attitudes in a manner favourable to it as to recommend something was to incite them to have similarly favourable attitudes; and it would be plausible to claim in each case that a mere understanding of language enables us to see this. Of these two possible enterprises the second may be possibly wrong in detail or even wholly misguided; but it is philosophical, whereas the first is hardly a part of philosophy even on a liberal view of its scope. We might indeed think it an advantage that we have to think in terms of action rather than emotion; for morality is surely primarily concerned with action, and if moral language is to be dynamic, as Stevenson maintained that it must be, there is no reason why its power should be exerted on our feelings rather than on our activities.

Thus our survey of the earlier attempts to define emotive meaning leads us to the conclusion that they were in many ways seriously defective. But we should do well not to think too lowly of these early versions of the emotive theory which we have so far been examining. They had the great merit of turning the philosophy of value to explore what were at that time totally neglected possibilities. The philosophers who produced these versions were mainly concerned to make the revolutionary suggestion that evaluative utterances were neither reports of the way the world investigated by scientists goes round, nor yet of the revolution of some transcendent world of values, but rather involved an utterly different use of language variously called emotive, magnetic or dynamic. They were at least clear, unlike the subjectivists, that in this use of language one was not reporting or describing the feelings and emotions that oneself and others had. Just as to say 'I promise' is to make a promise and not to report that one is making a promise, and just as to say 'I apologise' is to express one's regret and not to report that one is apologising or that one is feeling regret, so they were clear that they wanted to deny that to say that something was good was to report one's emotions or feeling or any other state of the universe. This is an exciting suggestion. We no doubt find that they failed to give a clear positive characterisation of this use of language in general; they had barely attempted to apply their view to solving the separate and special problems of ethics, aesthetics and allied fields. But we need scarcely wonder or complain about this. It will be more sensible to move on to examine some fuller and more carefully worked out versions of the theory.

4

STEVENSON'S ETHICS AND LANGUAGE

We now leave the earlier adumbrations of the emotive theory, and shall examine in some detail the views of Stevenson as set out in his *Ethics and Language*. No detailed, systematic exposition of Stevenson's views will be offered; a general acquaintance with them is presupposed. It will be more profitable to examine carefully his views on certain major issues, particularly where they seem to require supplementation or emendation. Since there will be a good deal of criticism on many points, I should like to say now, once for all, that I regard this book as a work of great value which contributed importantly to analytical ethics. I believe that a few serious mistakes led Stevenson consistently to distort his otherwise valuable insights, the most important of these mistakes being his explicit account of the nature of emotive meaning. We shall therefore do well to commence our examination of Stevenson's views by considering what he has to say on this topic.

Emotive meaning and attitudes

Stevenson's account of emotive meaning is wholly in causal terms, not inadvertently, but because he wishes to explain all meaning in causal terms. Thus on page 33 of the first edition of *Ethics and Language* he says: 'The emotive meaning of a word is the power that the word acquires, on account of its history in emotional situations, to evoke or directly express attitudes, as distinct from describing or designating them.' But, as shown in the preceding chapter, the power to evoke attitudes is a natural causal property; this is no less true because, according to Stevenson, a necessary condition of this power operating is that we should have been conditioned in a certain way. We have also seen, it is true, that the expression of attitudes, which Stevenson also brings in, is often a matter involving linguistic convention, when we express attitudes in words, and it is true that Stevenson allows to emotive meaning the expression of the attitude of the speaker. But this admission to emotive meaning of something like a conventional force as well as a natural power, which we at first might claim, is only apparent; for Stevenson wishes us, most unnaturally, to conceive of expressing in purely causal terms. Thus he says: 'Emotive meaning is a meaning in which the response (from the hearer's point of view) or the stimulus (from the speaker's point of view) is a range of emotions' (ibid., p. 59). Thus we are asked to believe that expressing emotion by means of a word with emotive meaning is to be caused to utter the word by the occurrence of the emotion in question.

It is crucial to grasp the implication of this causal theory. One implication is that evaluative language, language with emotive meaning, will be dynamic, will have emotive meaning, only for a hearer whose existing attitude requires changing, or, at least, confirming; for one cannot evoke in a hearer an attitude that he already fully shares. More importantly still, evaluative language will never be dynamic in any way in relation to the speaker; the use of the evaluative language is merely a result of or response to attitudes and emotions that he already has. Thus evaluative language, according to this theory, can never be self-directive; to tell oneself that one ought to act in a certain way will be a result of having already a favourable attitude towards so acting, not to give oneself a ground for so acting. Thus Stevenson's definition of emotive meaning more or less forces him to lay great weight on the role of evaluative language in changing the attitude of hearers; otherwise emotive language loses its *raison d'être*, for it ceases to be dynamic. But the dynamic, or, as he sometimes said, the magnetic, power of evaluative language was the thing on which in his earliest *Mind* article of 1937 he had already seized as crucial, beyond the power of 'propositional' ethics to explain.

I have no doubt that Stevenson's position would become more plausible if he abandoned his causal account of language in general and emotive language in particular. He could then replace the component in emotive meaning which he calls the power to evoke attitudes by a conventional force of commending and recommending attitudes; similarly the interpretation of the expression of an attitude in terms of a conditioned response could be replaced by a conventional force in virtue of which one manifested, announced and adopted attitudes. Such an account might well require modifications of comparative detail, but would have avoided mistakes of principle with far-reaching consequences, including those mentioned in the previous paragraph. Some of these consequences we must now trace.

Stevenson maintains, rightly I believe, that there is a kind of disagreement which he calls disagreement in attitude as distinct from disagreement in belief. If it be said that belief is itself an attitude, we can modify the foregoing and say that disagreement in the attitude of belief is not the only sort of disagreement in attitude. If we disagree about what play is on at the theatre, that is a disagreement in belief; if we agree what play is on, but you want us to go and I want us to stay away, that is a disagreement in attitude. Stevenson further holds that ethical and other evaluative disagreement is a species of disagreement in attitude, accompanied usually, but not necessarily, by disagreement in belief. Factual disagreements, on the contrary, involve disagreement only in belief. He also wishes to maintain that the feature of ethical statements in virtue of which ethical disagreement always includes disagreement in attitude is their possession of emotive meaning. Obviously, then, 'attitude' and 'emotion' are key words in Stevenson's vocabulary, and we should do well to look carefully at them.

The first point that should be made clear is that attitudes and emotions are much more different from each other than Stevenson's usual treatment of them would suggest. Both are indeed very different from belief, but this does not hinder them from being very different from each other. My attitude to something is not more or less the same thing as my emotional relation to it; one's emotions and attitude can indeed be in conflict, as when John is, say, strongly attracted towards Mary but, for some reason, maintains an aloof attitude towards her. Again, one may have an attitude towards an object to which one stands in no emotional relationship. This is perhaps necessarily true if one's attitude towards religion, say, or golf is one of complete indifference.

If, then, an attitude can be out of harmony with one's emotions, and if some attitudes have an absence of emotion as a prime feature, they must exhibit considerable differences. Let us consider attitudes first. The first thing to notice, and it is pretty obvious, is that while we may reconsider and change our attitudes from time to time they do not vary from minute to minute or hour to hour, as do our thoughts and feelings; this is not because they are simply tougher and more enduring, but because, while a change in the direction of our attention counts as the end of a train of thought or the subsidence of an emotion, it does not count as the end of an attitude. There is a category difference. Let us suppose that someone's attitude towards religion is one of complete indifference; it may remain so whether he thinks about golf or mathematics, whether he is asleep or awake, whether he feels gay, angry, tired or bored. What would, then, count as an end to the attitude of complete indifference to religion? It is not necessary that he should acquire some emotions of a religious or anti-religious character; for if he started to study religions and their history carefully but with emotional detachment that would count as the end of his attitude of indifference, which would have yielded to one of, say, uncommitted interest. Clearly, joining in religious practices, attacking religion at Hyde Park Corner and many other activities would also be incompatible with an attitude of indifference, in any but freak circumstances, and would manifest an attitude of acceptance or hostility. Certainly indifference, which is incompatible with having any strong emotions at the thought or mention of its object, is a very special case. But emotion is only one among the relevant factors in the case of any attitude, and always a factor which can be outweighed by others. One can, and often does, maintain a neutral, or even a favourable attitude towards an object which excites a strong emotional repugnance. Often it will be our duty, and within our power, to do this; it is likely in such circumstances for it also to be our duty to try to overcome the emotion, but we may not succeed. We can decide on our attitudes, but we can only take steps which are likely to result in a change of our emotions.

Emotions are, indeed, importantly relevant to our attitudes; but they are not predominantly or exceptionally relevant to them. Thoughts, beliefs, words and deeds are all also relevant, and will be expected, as a matter of logic and not merely of psychological appropriateness, to vary in character according as the attitude is one of interest, indifference, disdain, aloofness, friendliness, benevolence, hostility or, let us add, approval. But, though emotion, thought, word and deed are all logically relevant to the determination of an attitude, none is essential. If word and deed are in conflict with thought and feeling we may, according to differences in the situation very hard to make explicit, allow either word and deed or thought and feeling to be decisive. If a man is attracted by his neighbour's wife, but does not betray the fact ordinarily in word or in deed, then word and deed will prevail and we shall call his attitude one of aloofness, polite friendliness, or what have you. In different circumstances it will be the words and deeds that are discounted; the man is a hypocrite, pretending to an attitude which he does not really have. The degree to which emotion is important will vary from attitude to attitude. It might be odd to claim an attitude of repugnance to something which leaves one emotionally untouched; but many attitudes, including some moral ones, are very likely to be relatively unemotional. There are countless things in the world that meet with our approval or disapproval, no question of hypocrisy being involved, which do not touch our imaginations sufficiently to awaken any emotional response; evil institutions in far away countries, for example, meet with our moral condemnation but, since we are not confronted with their tragic effects, no emotional indignation; at a more pedestrian level, we all maintain friendly attitudes to people with complete sincerity without experiencing any emotional attachment. So, though we should recognise that certain attitudes demand an appropriate emotion, and that certain emotions go naturally with some attitudes, they do not in general play a preponderant role in attitudes, and certainly cannot be equated with them. From the moral point of view it is particularly important that we can often choose to maintain an attitude which is out of accord with our feelings and emotions.

Thus to ascribe to a person a certain attitude is to ascribe to him a certain pattern of thoughts, beliefs, feelings, emotions, words and deeds, and the relative importance of the various elements in the pattern will vary according to the particular character of the attitude. So long as the pattern continues to be manifested in his activities when circumstances are appropriate, so long does the attitude last.

Now our emotions are relatively beyond our control, completely so in the case of the less stable among us. We may try to suppress them, to discipline ourselves in ways which we expect to modify them, or to have them modified for us by psychotherapists; but we cannot simply choose which emotions to feel. We can, however, choose our words and our deeds, or most of us can most of the time. Because of this we can to a great extent choose our attitudes and thus be immediately responsible for them, particularly those attitudes to which word and deed are of paramount importance. This, in its turn, explains why we can and do speak quite naturally of people adopting attitudes and maintaining them, of people being argued out of them, of logically consistent and inconsistent sets of attitudes, of well-based and ill-considered attitudes, and so on. But we do not adopt or maintain our feelings and emotions; we are not argued out of them, even if we may be in some way talked out of them; though they may be appropriate, they can hardly be well-based.

The facts just presented are a selection from those that make it possible for us to speak of disagreement and agreement in attitude, as in belief, but not of agreement and disagreement in feelings and emotions. We can call certain differences in attitude disagreements precisely because we can maintain attitudes as we maintain beliefs, because we can be argued out of attitudes as we can be argued out of beliefs, because with reason given we can be expected to abandon attitudes as with reason given we can be expected to abandon beliefs. But we cannot, and do not, speak of disagreement in emotion or feeling precisely because we do not maintain emotions and feelings and cannot be argued out of them. We regularly speak rather of emotional compatibility and harmony, or incompatibility and disharmony, rather than of emotional disagreement. If this emotional incompatibility or disharmony arises we can go to psychiatrists for therapy or to such bodies as Marriage Guidance Councils for advice on how to surmount it, mitigate it, or, at the worst, live with it; but we cannot be argued out of it, even if we may choose to maintain a sensible attitude towards it and towards each other, in spite of it.

We need not attempt to deny that our attitudes are often influenced by our emotions. We may well fail to recognise the irrationality of our attitudes because they are emotionally attractive to us; strong feeling may also help us to maintain a well-considered attitude in the face of opposition. But this interaction in no way blurs the distinction to which we have drawn attention. It is, indeed, clear that our emotions may similarly influence our beliefs, as in the notorious case of wishful thinking; but this is no ground for assimilating beliefs to emotions.

When Stevenson insists that ethical and other evaluative disagreement always involves disagreement in attitude, not merely disagreement in belief, he does well. But to give this point its proper importance we must insist also on the difference between disagreement in attitude and emotional disharmony. This latter difference is blurred by the name 'the emotive theory of ethics', and Stevenson does not bring it out fully in *Ethics and Language*. Moral and other evaluation is not a matter of feeling and emotion alone, nor of dispositions to feel emotions, but of attitude. Certainly evaluation is not foreign to emotion, and we should naturally expect people to feel strongly on many evaluative issues. But it is of equal importance to observe that an evaluative judgement is liable to be made with prejudice and insufficient care when emotion is present in any great strength. We are rightly exhorted to keep emotion out of it for the time being when we are attempting to determine the proper attitude towards such issues as capital punishment.

When one wishes to change a person's evaluative attitude one does not wish to change only, or most importantly, his emotions, but rather the whole pattern of his thinking and behaviour. Certainly one may try to accomplish this by working on his emotions, borrowing the art of the demagogue and the advertising agent; while it may not always be improper to do this, it surely involves treating him as less than rational and is not to be ventured on lightly. That emotion may influence attitudes no more shows their identity than does the fact that emotion may influence belief demonstrate the identity of belief and emotion. Sometimes, indeed, any significant degree of emotion would be absurdly out of place as an accompaniment to an evaluative attitude. Thus one may evaluate one type of power shovel or insecticide more highly than another; if someone disagrees with us we shall have a case of disagreement in attitude. But we should appear ridiculous if we were to allow our disagreement to become in any way emotional; only a fanatic will feel emotionally committed to a design for power shovels.

Thus I believe that Stevenson does an injustice to the best elements in his own view by not making clearer the difference between disagreement in attitude and emotional disharmony or incompatibility. Sometimes he seems hardly to discriminate between the two. The main ground for alleging this confusion is, of course, that Stevenson speaks of the emotive use of language as being (causally) concerned with the exhibition and induction of attitudes. If, in using emotive language we are, as Stevenson claims (ibid., p. 59), evoking a response or exhibiting a response which is a range of emotions, it is not intelligible how one could think emotive language especially suitable to changing moral and other evaluative attitudes unless one more or less identified an attitude with a range of emotions. Why, indeed, accept the name 'emotive language' to characterise evaluative terms unless one thinks that evaluation is at least primarily an emotional response?

It would be false to say that Stevenson shows no awareness of any difference between mere emotional states and attitudes. In fairness we should quote extensively from the most important passage in which he distinguishes them:

'The term "emotion" is introduced temporarily, since the term "emotive" suggests it; but hereafter it will be convenient to replace "emotion" by "feeling or attitude"—both to preserve terminological uniformity throughout the book and to emphasise an important distinction. The term "feeling" is to be taken as designating an affective state that reveals its full nature to immediate introspection, without use of induction. An attitude, however, is more complicated than that, as our previous examples will have suggested. It is, in fact, itself a complicated conjunction of dispositional properties (for dispositions are ubiquitous throughout all psychology), marked by stimuli and responses which relate to hindering or assisting whatever it is that is called the "object" of the attitude. A precise definition of "attitude" is too difficult a matter to be attempted here; hence the term, central though it is to the present work, must for the most part be understood from its current usage, and from the usage of the many terms ("desire", "wish", "disapproval", etc.) which name specific attitudes. Meanwhile it is important to see that immediate feelings are more simple than attitudes, and that attitudes must not, amid temptations to hypostatise, be confused with them.' (ibid., p. 60).

But even here the distinction is left as being one merely of simplicity and complication. The passage quoted fails to bring out the differences between feeling and attitude that are crucial for the analysis of moral thinking. Attitudes are still merely a matter of stimulus and response, differing from feeling only by being a complicated conjunction of dispositions. No attempt is made to bring out the differences, some of which we have noted, which make attitudes a field of potential agreement and disagreement, whereas with feeling we have nothing but compatability and incompatibility, harmony and disharmony. Moreover if the term 'emotive' suggests the term 'emotion', which is misleading, why was it itself ever introduced? Incidentally, one might note that wishes and desires are very odd examples to give as paradigms of attitudes, even if they be complicated conjunctions of dispositions; to wish for a cup of tea, for example, is hardly to have an attitude towards it. What is important to stress is that while, at least in the short run, we cannot help what we desire, it makes sense to speak of adopting an attitude, modifying it, abandoning it and the like—the sorts of thing that make us responsible for having the attitudes we do in a way that we cannot be responsible for our desires.

Stevenson also says that: 'it will be recalled that an attitude is a *disposition* to act in certain ways and to experience certain feelings, rather than itself a certain action or feeling'. It is the word 'disposition' that is italicised; but is not dispositions that we adopt and are argued out of; indeed, our attitude to a certain matter may be such that we have to check our natural dispositions to action. Thus it does seem that Stevenson tends to underestimate or to misrepresent the difference between mere feelings and attitudes; the distinction which he does emphasise, that of complication, is not the important one to bring out. His willingness at times to neglect the distinction altogether perhaps arises from a failure to see why it is important.

We have so far in this chapter observed that Stevenson defines emotive meaning in terms of the *de facto* power of terms that have it to produce and be produced by feelings and attitudes. We have also seen that he distinguishes between feelings and attitudes only by making attitudes a complicated set of dispositions to states of mind rather than a state of mind itself. These two views, erroneous if what we are calling 'emotive meaning' is to be the distinctive feature of evaluative language in general, are intimately connected. If evaluations are causally related, essentially, to attitudes, and attitudes are like feelings except in complication, then, since feelings can be altered by talk only as a matter of rhetoric, only by some natural power as opposed to some conventional meaning, the characteristic feature of evaluative discourse should indeed be diagnosed purely in terms of power to evoke a response. Here we have already the key to three very serious defects in Stevenson's views. We shall have to discuss each in detail later, but they may now be briefly catalogued.

(1) If to use evaluative language is merely to bring causally efficacious means of change to bear on attitudes and feelings there can be no discrimination of valid and invalid argument in evaluation. Any support must be causal reinforcement or persuasion.

(2) Similarly, there can be no distinction of logically relevant and irrelevant consideration in arriving at any evaluation; there will be only that which carries a persuasive influence and that which does not.

(3) Since evaluative language is conceived of as designed to change attitudes, and perhaps to reinforce them, we have the odd consequence that there would be no use for evaluative language in fields where stable agreement was known to exist; when used successfully it renders itself henceforth superfluous. Stevenson gives evaluative language the sole end of attaining agreement in attitude and allowing no use for it when agreement has been attained. There will always be evaluative propaganda, but no evaluative information. But it is very odd to suppose that I would say to you 'This is good cheese' only in order to change your attitude towards it; one would more often say this sort of thing just to tell someone else what the cheese is like when he does not know, being helpful rather than a propagandist.

These three features of Stevenson's views, all surely highly implausible, are not mere aberrations on Stevenson's part; they essentially follow from his understanding of evaluative language and attitudes.

The attitude of approval
The attitudes which are treated as being of greatest importance in Stevenson's account of evaluative language are those of approval and disapproval. It will be rewarding to examine what account he gives of these attitudes.

In providing a model of the use of 'good' in such sentences as

'This is good', Stevenson suggests (ibid., p. 21) as a first pattern of analysis 'I approve of this, do so as well'. Here the first clause is said to give the descriptive component in the meaning of 'This is good' and the second—'do so as well'—to bring out, though inadequately, the emotive meaning.

It is the first clause—'I approve of this'—that we are now to try to elucidate. Here are four quotations from Stevenson about it.

(1) It is a 'declarative statement . . . which describes the attitude of the speaker'. (ibid., p. 22)

(2) It is an 'introspective report . . . describing his state of mind'. (ibid., p. 25)

(3) 'It makes an assertion about the speaker's state of mind, and like any psychological statement, is open to empirical confirmation or disconfirmation, whether introspective or behavioristic.' (ibid., p. 26)

(4) 'One must take care, for instance, before concluding:

'(a) If any person says that he approves of anything, then he *implies* that it is good, provided, of course, that "good" is used by *him*, and so refers to *his* approval only.

'It may be objected: "But people often want to say that they approve of something *without* implying that it is good; they may wish to indicate their approval as a mere fact about themselves, leaving any discussion about what is good for another time." This is quite true, even for those who follow the first pattern; but it is readily explained. "Good" is emotively strong in a way that "approve" is not. A person does not proceed from "I approve of this" to "This is good", accordingly, unless he wishes (as he sometimes may not) to recommend the object in question to his hearers. Now (a) above seems to require a person to go from the one statement to the other, as a matter of mere logic; whereas it obviously does not require this so long as the latter is emotively more active. Hence (a) is very likely to be misleading, even though (for the first pattern only, and disregarding emotive meaning) it is logically correct.' (ibid., p. 105).

These four passages show that Stevenson regards 'I approve of this' as being purely factual or 'descriptive', lacking the degree of emotive meaning that makes 'This is good', in contrast, evaluative.

This view of Stevenson's is very hard to accept. In view of the great interest philosophers have always shown in the relation of approval to goodness, we had better make a careful investigation into the concept of approval on our own account before continuing with the examination of Stevenson's views. Stevenson is, of course, far from being alone in regarding 'I approve' as a statement of fact, as psychological biography. It is a very common view, but we may confine our attention to Stevenson and Ayer, who both accept the view but draw very different consequences from it.

On the ground that 'I approve' is purely descriptive Ayer rejects the view that 'I approve of this' means the same as 'This is good'. For if 'I approve of this' is a mere statement of fact (descriptive in meaning), we shall be open, he holds, to the usual objections to the naturalistic fallacy if we try to define 'good' in terms of 'approval'. Thus in *Language, Truth and Logic* he says: 'We reject . . . the subjectivist view that a man who asserts that a certain act is right, or that a certain thing is good, is saying that he himself approves of it, on the ground that a man who confessed that he sometimes approved of what was bad or wrong would not be contradicting himself' (2nd ed., p. 104). But this argument of Ayer's is neither a proper application of the argument against the naturalistic fallacy, nor has it any other kind of merit. It is without merit because, if the fact that a man could confess that he sometimes approved of what was bad or wrong without contradicting himself proves that 'I approve of this' is not identical in meaning with 'This is good', we can prove by parity of argument that 'I approve of this' is not identical in meaning with 'I approve of this'. For a person could easily enough confess that he sometimes approved of what he does not now approve of without contradicting himself. Ayer, at best (and no doubt), disproves the view that 'This is good' means the same as 'I sometimes approve of this'; but 'I sometimes approve of this' is surely importantly different from 'I (now) approve of this'.

Ayer's argument which we have just controverted is not a version of the argument against naturalism, because that takes the form 'X is not identical with Y since one can deny that an X is Y without contradiction'. So, to use the naturalistic fallacy argument against the view that 'This is good' means the same as 'I approve of this', Ayer would have to claim that one could say 'I approve of this but it is not good', or 'This is good but I do not approve of it' without self-contradiction. But surely it is very plausible indeed to hold that someone who says either 'This is good but I do not approve of it' or 'I approve of this but it is not good' *is* contradicting himself? It would certainly be a very puzzling thing to say and would require a good deal of explanation to make intelligible. Perhaps one could say something of this sort in a context in which one thinks that the thing is good in certain respects or from a certain point of view, but disapproves of it in another respect or from another point of view; thus one might think that one should not use good (= high-quality) paper for making rough notes and therefore approve of some paper (for making notes) although, or because, it is not good paper. But then in such a context one might equally say 'This is good paper (for making notes) but it is not good paper (from the point of view of the connoisseur in paper)'. But, if we put such confusing, though intelligible, uses of language on one side, there is obviously a great deal of oddity in a person's saying that something is good but he does not approve of it; moreover, it is logically perplexing rather than psychologically implausible. So if Ayer had in fact made use of the argument he claimed to use he would have chosen a far from convincing occasion to do so.

Why should there be this intimate link between 'This is good' and 'I approve of this' if the former is evaluative and the latter, as both Ayer and Stevenson claim, purely descriptive? Stevenson claims to answer this question. Though he holds, as we have already observed in the passages quoted above, that we cannot maintain that 'I approve of X and X is bad' is always a contradiction, 'it lends itself to this interpretation unless explanatory remarks are made'. This is, he holds, because 'I approve' represents the descriptive component in the meaning of 'good'. He can maintain this in spite of his general acceptance of Moore's attack on the naturalistic fallacy by claiming that 'good' has in addition an emotive meaning; Moore is right in denying that 'I approve of this' means the same as 'This is good', while wrong in thinking that 'good' must therefore have some other descriptive meaning. Thus Stevenson finds an intimate link, descriptive meaning, between 'This is good' and 'I approve of this'.

We must come back later to the full doctrine of Stevenson. Meanwhile we note that Ayer and Stevenson agree that 'I approve' is autobiography, pure description of a state of mind or attitude or emotion (exactly what is a point not now at issue). Are they right in what they are agreed upon? To decide this let us look at some of the uses of 'approve' for ourselves.

First we must distinguish (a) 'approve' with a direct object and (b) 'approve of', as in the following examples:

(a1) I approve this application
(b1) I approve of this application

(a2) The Minister approved the application
(b2) The Minister approved of the application

The difference between (a) and (b) is demonstrated by the fact that in each pair of examples above the (a) and (b) examples are logically independent, neither implying nor excluding the other. I may approve of an application which I cannot approve because I lack the authority to do so, while the Minister may approve an application under political pressure which he thoroughly disapproves of.

If we consider the simple 'I approve' first, it is clear that in the first person present it is a pure performative in Austin's sense. To say 'I (hereby) approve the application' is to approve it. It is the sort of thing that officials have constantly to do, but ordinary mortals rarely. 'He approved the application' and similar utterances are clearly historical reports of the performance of an act of approval, whether by uttering the words 'I approve' or otherwise. But the pure performative is not a report and therefore not a candidate for being the descriptive element in the sentence 'This is good'; it is not the description of one's own state of mind or attitude or emotions or what you will. There is, no doubt, in many circumstances a fair inductive inference to some favourable attitude of the official who says 'I approve', but it is uncertain. There is, perhaps, some sort of logical tie between the performative 'I approve' and a favourable attitude; it might be inexplicable why we have the device if officials did not normally have a favourable attitude to applications that they approved; but clearly some may all the time and all may some of the time have an unfavourable attitude to what they approve without any oddness.

But no one, happily, has suggested that 'This is good' should be analysed in terms of the pure performative 'I approve', though many of us from time to time fail to distinguish it with sufficient clarity from 'I approve of'. This is clearly the interesting expression and we may turn to it now without more ado.

Is 'approve of' purely descriptive as Ayer and Stevenson once said and some eminent authorities still say (for example, R. B. Brandt, in his *Ethical Theory* of 1959 at least implies this on page 209)? Stevenson can himself be brought as witness to the contrary, as will now be shown.

Stevenson introduced the notion of disagreement in attitude into moral philosophy, though not of course into common speech where it already existed, unused by moral philosophers. But we should note that not every time when two people differ in attitude to-wards the same object do they also disagree in attitude. Presumably every man's attitude towards his wife ought to be different from every other man's attitude towards her; but this is not a way of saying that every man ought to disagree in attitude with all other men on at least one topic. In fact, a disagreement of a practical nature is more likely to arise if someone else has too similar an attitude towards the wife. Similarly, it seems appropriate that the attitudes of a native towards his own country's problems should be in many respects different from that of a foreigner.

Clearly, then, not every difference in attitude is a disagreement, and we shall shortly offer a tentative general criterion to distinguish

the two types of situation. But for immediate purposes it is sufficient
for us to claim that when of two persons one approves and the
other disapproves of the very same thing this, at least, is a case of
disagreement in attitude. But if this is so then Stevenson, who regards disagreement in attitude as closely tied to emotive meaning,
must surely allow that the utterances 'I approve of this' and 'I disapprove of this' are not purely descriptive in meaning. He certainly
seems to allow that we do here have a case of disagreement in
attitude. Thus he says (op. cit., p. 22) of A and B who say 'This is
good' and 'I fully concur' that 'here the declarative part of the
remarks ['I approve' and 'I concur in approving'], testifying to
convergent attitudes, are sufficient to imply the agreement [in
attitude]'. But he tends to speak as though ' "I approve"—"I
also" ' and ' "I approve"—"I do not" ' testify to or report an
agreement or disagreement rather than expressing it; perhaps he
regards this as marking a difference from cases where there is explicit disagreement about goodness which do constitute disagreement in attitude. But this, if he holds it, is not a tenable view. If one
says to a third party 'A approves of the arrangement, but I do not'
this is indeed to report or testify to a disagreement; but this disagreement may well have taken the form of one of us saying 'I
approve of it' and the other 'I do not'. One's remark to the third
party is not a report of a report of a disagreement in such a case.
Very often the way in which we come out publicly in favour of
something is by saying that we approve of it; it is a mistake to
construe such utterances as reports of a private coming out in
favour from which we can infer with some confidence that the
utterer is willing to come out in favour publicly by some other
method. So if Stevenson is right, as I think he is, in claiming that
disagreement in attitude is a mark of there being more than merely
factual disagreement we must conclude that expressions of approval
and disapproval are not merely factual, or 'declarative'.

How can A and B maintain quite different attitudes towards A's
wife without there being any disagreement involved? Let us
suppose that A's attitude is one of intimate affection and B's one of
polite civility, which may well involve no disagreement. These are

both perfectly proper attitudes, given the facts of the case. The important thing here seems to be that the difference in attitude need not arise from, and certainly does not mark or express, any difference in evaluation of the wife. A will not on this account have grounds for complaining that B estimates his wife less highly than he himself does. Similarly, if A has an attitude of eager interest in modern music while B is indifferent to it, this will not constitute a disagreement if the difference arises from B being tone-deaf rather than from a different evaluation of the music.

But when a difference in attitude does involve a disagreement, as in the cases of respect and disrespect, admiration and disdain, like and dislike, approval and disapproval, there seems always to be present an element of favourable or unfavourable evaluation which is absent from the differences which do not constitute disagreements. Respect, admiration and approval are all favourable, and their opposites are unfavourable. But I cannot neutrally report that I have a favourable attitude to something, as I can neutrally report an attitude that is neither favourable nor unfavourable. 'I have no intention of exhibiting any favour towards it, but I will just let you know, as a mere report, that I admire (approve of, like) it' will not do, for it is self-defeating. The favour exhibited may be unimportant in the context, but it is present. Unlike 'He approves of (admires, likes) it', 'I approve of (admire, like) it' is, in itself, as we naturally say, an expression of approval, liking or admiration, and this is why it differs from the third person utterance, which is a mere report, in basic character and 'feel'. Consequently, when Stevenson says in a passage already quoted (ibid., p. 105) that people 'may wish to indicate their approval as a mere fact about themselves, leaving any discussion about what is good for another time', we should simply and flatly reply that this cannot be done. We have yet to consider whether 'I approve of this' is altogether identical in content with 'This is good', but it certainly does not leave the question of merit quite undiscussed.

There is no mystery here. If we remember that an attitude is manifested in words and deeds, among other ways, then we can regard an avowal of approval, of liking, or of admiration as one of the uses of words whereby the attitude is manifested or expressed. It might, indeed, be held that it manifests the attitude in a more direct way than do most other forms of behaviour; it is plausible to hold that the major role of such a locution as 'I approve of this' is to manifest or express the attitude in question. Other behaviour which may make an attitude of approval manifest, such as acting in favour of it rather than against it, could hardly be said to have this manifestation of the attitude as its main point.

George Pitcher, in an article entitled 'On Approval' in the *Philosophical Review* for 1958, makes a number of other important and relevant points about approval which need, therefore, to be mentioned here only in summary fashion.

(a) He maintains that one can approve of something only if and in so far as it is subject to human control. Thus one cannot approve of the Atlantic ocean or of Arcturus.

(b) He maintains that one must not merely be in favour of the object approved of, a point which we have already insisted on; one must also have reasons for doing so. One can say 'I just happen to like this (him), but I do not know why', but one is not entitled to say 'I just happen to approve of this, but I do not know why'.

(c) Moreover, Pitcher claims, one must not merely have some reasons for approving of something, they must be the right kind of reasons. Pitcher says (loc. cit., p. 207) that 'approval is intrinsically general'. The principle reason he gives for this is that if one approves of anything for a reason this reason must be acceptable to you also as a reason for approving of anything else to which it is applicable; but this seems to be a lapse; for what he says applies to all reasons for anything and not merely to reasons for approving. If I happen to give a reason for liking something it must also be accepted by me as a reason (though not necessarily a sufficient reason) for liking anything else to which it is applicable. The reason why approval is intrinsically general is that one must have reasons for it, whereas one need have no reasons for liking. But it does also seem to be true, as Pitcher claims, that some reasons for favouring things in some way, such as liking them, are not possible reasons for approving of them. Thus, if someone said that he disapproved of meat-eating, the ground that it was unhealthy or barbaric would be of the right sort, even if false; but that he did not like the taste of meat would be no reason at all for disapproving of it, even if true.

(d) One must think that anyone in the same position ought also to approve of what one approves of oneself. Thus one could say to one's successor in an office that one liked to do things in a certain way, while recognising that he might not and that it was a matter of taste. But one could not treat the methods of procedure which one approved of as a mere matter of taste; if the successor does not share the approval one or the other is wrong.

This examination of approval, though no doubt exhausting, has been by no means exhaustive; there remain loose ends. But certain things, at least, are already clear. First, whether somebody approves of something cannot be a mere matter of simply observable behaviour or introspectible feeling; however a person feels and behaves, we cannot count that as being sufficient grounds for holding that he approves of something, since, in addition, the behaviour and feelings must be logically appropriate as fulfilling the sort of criteria that Pitcher mentions. Logically, my feelings may be as surprising and my behaviour as eccentric as one cares to imagine, but I cannot just happen to approve of something which I know to be within no agent's control, can give no reasons for, and expect no one else to approve of. To say that one approves of something involves an implied claim that some such conditions as those specified by Pitcher are satisfied. To approve of something is not just to have a certain feeling, nor just to behave in a certain way; it is not even just to have a favourable attitude, but to have the special favourable attitude that satisfies these conditions.

Let us now return to the question of the relationship between 'I approve of this' and 'This is good'. We can now see at once that we cannot accept Ayer's argument that they cannot have the same or similar meanings because the one is purely descriptive, the other purely emotive; nor can we accept Stevenson's claim that, though it is the descriptive component of 'This is good', 'I approve of this' lacks the emotive meaning which the other has. We can see that we must disagree with both because we must deny that 'I approve of this' has the character which they both suppose it to have. Surely it is now clear that, if we accept the unfortunate expression 'has emotive meaning' as the conventional name for the special characteristic possessed by 'This is good' but not by purely factual (descriptive) statements, then we must acknowledge that 'I approve of this' has also got emotive meaning in its own right.

So far we have no grounds for distinguishing the characters of the two utterances under discussion. Indeed, we find that all save one of Pitcher's criteria for the legitimacy of saying 'I approve of this' are also criteria for the legitimacy of 'This is good'. In both cases one must be in favour of the object in question, one must have reasons for so being, they must be the right sort of reasons (what we said about appropriate reasons for expressing disapproval of meat-eating applies equally to asserting that it is bad), and finally, like 'I approve of this', 'This is good' cannot be used as a mere expression of personal taste which demands no agreement from others. Thus we have so far a number of reasons for assimilating 'This is good' to 'I approve of this'; are they then virtually identical in character?

It seems clear that they are not identical in meaning for two quite different reasons, each important and illuminating positively. First, though we cannot say, without absurdity, 'I approve of this, but it is not good', we may well say, and are often in a position of ignorance when we ought to say, 'I approve of this, but perhaps it is not good'. But we cannot say 'I approve of this, but perhaps I do not'. This, on its own, disposes of the thesis of strict identity. It seems that 'This is good' is more like 'It is correct (in a sense of 'correct' in which it is opposed to 'mistaken') to approve of this'. Thus 'I approve of this, but maybe it is not good' can be assimilated to 'I approve of this, but maybe mistakenly'. To say that something is good will, looked at this way, differ from saying that one approves of it mainly in that it will be more impersonal, will exclude the possibility that the reasons that one has for approval are mistaken or outweighed by other considerations, and the like. Holloway offered a very relevant and helpful analogy in an article entitled 'Ethical Qualities', in *The Proceedings of the Aristotelian Society* for 1947–8, which we may adapt for our purposes. We may compare, in certain limited respects, 'This is good' to 'This is terrifying', and 'I approve of this' to 'I am frightened of this'. Given the pairs of utterances 'This is terrifying—I am frightened of this' and 'This is good—I approve of this', we can in each case hardly assert one of the members of a pair while denying the other; but we can say 'I approve of this, but it may not really be good' and we can say 'I am frightened of this but maybe it is not genuinely terrifying'. 'Terrifying' seems to resemble 'correctly to be feared', as 'good' seems to resemble 'correctly to be approved of'. In both cases the impersonal form seems to differ from the personal by excluding the possibility of mistake. 'It is certain' shows a similar variation from 'I am certain'. We may also take a hint from the line taken by G. E. Moore in his 'Reply to my Critics' which appeared in *The Philosophy of G. E. Moore* (p. 538 ff.). We may take 'I think that *p*' and '*p*' as a pair of assertions to compare with 'I approve of this' and 'This is good'. It is not the case that 'I think that *p*' entails '*p*' or *vice versa*, and it is not true that 'I approve of this' entails 'This is good' or *vice versa* (which is one reason why 'I approve of this' is not even a part (the 'descriptive' part) of the meaning of 'This is good'); but it is the case that in saying 'I think that *p*' I imply, cautiously, that *p*, and that in saying '*p*' I imply that I think that *p;* similarly we may hold that 'I approve of this' and 'This is good' are not mutually entailing, but that in asserting either of them I always imply the other.

The other reason for denying the identity in meaning of 'I approve of this' and 'This is good' is quite different in character, and, indeed, involves us in modifying what we have so far allowed to pass. It has two facets. First, as Pitcher pointed out (loc. cit., p. 210), sometimes it is correct to say that something is good but impossible to say that we approve of it, because it is not a proper object of approval. Thus rain on thirsty land is, no doubt, a good thing, and earthquakes are no doubt bad things, but I cannot approve of the one or disapprove of the other, just as I cannot approve of the Atlantic ocean. But in each case one could say 'I welcome the rain' and 'I deplore the earthquake', which will have a similar relation to the impersonal statements of goodness and badness in this sort of context to that which statements of approval and disapproval have to them in their appropriate kind of context. We can say only that the relationship is similar, not that it is the same; for 'I welcome this' and 'I deplore this' are pure performatives having no truth value, unlike 'I approve of this'. We shall also find contexts in which, while 'I approve of' may not be impossible, it will be a less appropriate personal correlate of the impersonal judgement of goodness than, say, 'I commend' or 'I recommend'. Thus we see that approval is only one of a number of attitudes which, varying with the context, are all equally implied by judgements of goodness. The second facet of this argument is the converse of the former, that 'This is good' is not always the appropriate impersonal correlate of 'I approve of this'. If one person says 'Capital punishment is wrong' and a second replies 'Well, I wholly approve of it', is not this answer more nearly equivalent to 'It is right' than to 'It is good'? This may be accepted, but still seem a mere refinement of unimportant detail, if, like Stevenson (op. cit., p. 97), one regards 'right' and 'good' as near-synonyms. But reasons will, later in this book, be given for regarding 'right' and 'good' as belonging to quite distinct branches of practical language; if these reasons are cogent the point just made will not be unimportant.

Thus, apart from the fact that 'I approve of' is personal and 'good' is impersonal we find that they differ also by being in different ways relatively specialised and unspecialised. 'I approve' is specialised, along with 'I commend (recommend, welcome, reprobate, condemn, etc.)', 'This is good' being the relatively unspecialised impersonal correlate of them all. We have also relatively specialised impersonal forms like *admirable, commendable, praiseworthy*, etc. On the other hand and in another way 'approve of' is relatively unspecialised, covering questions of both goodness and rightness.

One final point, before we leave the topic of the relation of approval to goodness. It has often been maintained that there is another reason for holding 'I approve of this' to be very different from 'This is good'; this is that the latter stands to the former in the relation of a ground, without which the approval would be irrational. But surely the reasons that can sensibly be given for approving of something are of a quite different character from the claim that it is good; we should expect rather 'It will help to slow down inflation' and the like. In fact to offer 'Because it is good' as an answer to the question 'Why do you approve of this?' is to give too good an answer. As a piece of ungracious lifemanship such an answer could be classed with such retorts as 'Because I do', or even 'Mind your own business'.

There still are other difficulties about the relation of goodness to approval, commendation and the like. Some, at least, of them are discussed in Chapter 11.

5

STEVENSON'S ETHICS AND LANGUAGE

(continued)

It will be recollected that Stevenson claimed that we could regard 'I approve of this—please do so as well' as being a reasonably faithful analysis of 'This is good', 'I approve of this' being the purely declarative element and 'please do so as well' representing very crudely the emotive element. It may be useful to summarise our criticisms of this analysis, on the basis of the argumentation through which we have struggled, before proceeding to further issues. Here is such a summary under four heads.

(1) Stevenson gives his account of the special feature of evaluative utterances in terms of emotive meaning. But he construes this in terms of the mere causal efficacy of certain words to produce certain feelings and attitudes in hearers, and of such feelings and attitudes to stimulate certain words in speakers. He thus makes emotive meaning something altogether different from a use of words in accordance with a linguistic rule or convention, which is usually essential to meaning. Therefore emotive meaning is outside the cognisance of logic, and Stevenson will be unable to recognise logical relationships between evaluative utterances and others, or to distinguish valid from invalid arguments in favour of evaluations.

(2) In so far as the special feature of evaluative judgements can be called 'emotive meaning', 'I approve of this' has got emotive meaning quite as much as 'This is good', to which it is in many

ways very similar. Therefore it is not the declarative (descriptive, cognitive, factual) element in 'This is good'.

(3) But, as Stevenson at least partly realises, 'emotive meaning' is not a good name for this special feature of evaluative judgements. They express attitudes rather than emotions, and an attitude of approval need be in no way emotional. It will often be more acceptable if it is not.

(4) Stevenson makes the whole emotive meaning lie in the appeal to the hearer, 'Please do so as well'. But it would seem that the peculiar characteristic common to all evaluative judgements is rather that they manifest, express or proclaim the speaker's policy or attitude. In the case of such evaluations as 'This is nice' and 'I like this' perhaps there is only an expression of the speaker's favour, without any suggestion that others should share it. In so far as it is the case that 'This is good' and 'I approve of this' do solicit the agreement of others, it is because we are entitled to use such language only if our attitude is a reasoned one, so that divergence from it may count as disagreement. Since in these cases we should be prepared to defend our attitude as correct and rational, we thereby imply that any other attitude would be incorrect and irrational. But if we make the evaluative judgement 'I like this' there is no such implication, but at the most a vague, inductive presumption that as all human beings have much in common the other chap may well like it also. Thus Stevenson misrepresents the general character of evaluative utterances and also the reason why in some cases, only, there is an implication that the hearer should agree.

Stevenson's relativism

It is no part of the programme of this book to expound in detail the views which Stevenson so ably expressed for himself. But it will be useful now to state in summary form certain features of Stevenson's views as he gives them in chapters V to VII of *Ethics and Language*. They are chosen as being relevant to the issues now to be discussed, not in order to give a satisfactory conspectus of Stevenson's argument.

(1) When someone says that something is good he does no more than express his own personal approval in words which are also calculated to arouse the approval of his hearers.

(2) When people disagree in attitude, in spite of the emotive force of the emotive language which they use, it will often secure agreement in attitude if agreement in belief is obtained by the usual methods of rational argument and investigation appropriate to settling issues of fact. But there is no logical reason of any sort why agreement on any facts whatsoever should secure agreement in attitude. It is merely a well-founded psychological observation that agreement in attitude can often be arrived at in this way.

(3) No fact is logically more relevant to a disagreement in attitude than any other fact. It is merely a well-founded psychological observation that agreement on some facts is more likely to be effective in certain types of situation than agreement on other facts. Thus agreement on facts about a certain cow is more likely to secure agreement that it is a good cow than agreement on facts about ancient history.

(4) There can be no distinction between valid and invalid arguments from facts to evaluations. Anyone who attempts such a distinction will be 'selecting those inferences to which he is psychologically disposed to give assent, and perhaps inducing others to give a similar assent to them' (ibid., p. 171). But Stevenson, it should be added, does not regard all ways of securing agreement in attitude as being in all respects of equal merit.

On all these four points I believe Stevenson to be mistaken. It would be premature to make a final judgement before we have examined the second pattern of analysis, which is given to supplement the avowedly one-sided first pattern. But, proceeding provisionally to criticism, I wish to suggest that all these tenets stem from a single error, that of failure to distinguish between the setting of standards of evaluation and evaluation making use of those standards. Behind this, no doubt, lurks the fundamental error of the definition of evaluative force in purely causal terms, but we cannot continually hark back to that point. If this criticism is to be sustained, we must now expound the distinction between standard setting and standard using, in order to apply it to Stevenson's discussion. The distinction will be made in terms of the evaluation of kinds of things like cheese, apples and radio sets, not in terms of specifically ethical evaluation. I no longer believe that the distinction thus made can be applied without modification to the case of moral evaluation, as I used to believe, for reasons to be given in Chapter 9. But the required modifications do not affect the present issue materially, nor is Stevenson concerned only with moral evaluation.

From time to time and from place to place, when there is a bewildering variety of products of a certain kind upon the market, especially if these products are of importance to the community, then either the government or a manufacturers' association, or some body especially concerned with such matters, such as, in Britain, the British Standards Institution, will set up a research committee with the task of setting standards for the kind of product in question. Let us suppose that the product in question is cheese, and that a committee of people with much experience of cheese is convened to set up standards for cheese. In practice their task will be very complicated, since to some extent they will have to consider separately cheeses intended for cooking, grating, sandwich-making, etc., etc.; but we may simplify the matter to indicate the principles. These experts will, doubtless, have their individual preferences and will suggest as standards those features in cheese which they themselves like to find in cheese. One will suggest that a really good cheese should be regarded as one which possesses the characteristics ABCDE to a preeminent degree, and that cheeses which do not have these characteristics to the degree p should be regarded as being below market standard. Another expert will advocate as standards ABCFG instead of ABCDE, another BCDGH, another ACDEG, and so on. All, we must insist, will be saying: 'This is what *should* count as a standard-satisfying cheese'; they cannot be saying: 'This *is* what counts as a standard-satisfying cheese', since, *ex hypothesi*, there are in their social milieu as yet no standards in existence. All will be making their proposals on

c

the basis of their own personal preferences and their beliefs about
the preferences of others. Now maybe all will make slightly different
proposals (if they are very different there will be no hope for anything better than an inconclusive set of minority reports). But
they may be able to agree, all the same, in the interest of having
what all will agree to be a satisfactory, if not an ideal, set of standards
to use, to sink their differences and to accept some set of standards
for good cheese. But if this success is achieved we have now got a
totally new situation. In establishing the standards the experts were
expressing individual preferences, persuading and exhorting, in
addition to settling various factual questions, such as how long
cheese like this or like that would keep. But once there is agreement
standards have been set, and they can use them. When they now
speak of a good cheese they are not expressing a personal preference
or persuading others to have the same; they are evaluating in
accordance with agreed and accepted inter-subjective standards.
There would be no point in standard setting unless this stage
followed. Moreover, what facts it is relevant to mention in establishing whether a certain cheese is good or not is determined by no
estimates of psychological effectiveness but by what the standards
are. If fat-content is one, then it is relevant to mention fat-content,
and if not, not. If high fat-content is one standard, then 'This cheese
has a high fat-content and is therefore, *ceteris paribus*, good' will
be a valid argument, and if not, not. The crucial point is that in
standard setting they were saying 'This ought to be a standard for
good cheese'; afterwards they are judging, in accordance with the
accepted standards, 'This is good (bad) cheese'; there is no longer
any reason to persuade anybody of anything.

For standards to be used they must be accepted. But acceptance
need not be enthusiastic. 'This is, by conventional standards, good'
is no doubt something less than a genuine evaluation, though even
it can be of use in forming evaluative judgements for those who do
accept the conventional standards and judge the speaker reliable.
One who speaks thus usually has some other proposed standards
up his sleeve. But a grocer's assistant who dislikes all cheese may
say 'Yes, madam, this is excellent cheese' quite reliably, without any

desire to see cheese standards altered, and with no sneer whatever
in his tone of voice. Most of us accept most standards in most fields
without either question or fervour.

Our example of standard setting was highly schematic. Moreover most officially laid down standards are not pioneer steps but
rather attempts to make vague standards already in existence sufficiently precise for legal purposes. When the British Standards
Institution laid down standards for recorders (in about 1965)
people were already in agreement what a good recorder was like.
In most fields of evaluation there are no officially laid down
standards at all. Standards are gradually evolved and gradually
change, which means that the distinction between standard setting
and standard using can be blurred in practice. When an advertis-
ment gives 'six reasons why Bubblezone is better than any other
detergent' it may be hard for us to decide how far this is standard
using and how far an attempt to set standards by pretending that
they exist already. But the distinction is always there, and very
often there is no doubt what is at issue. The likelihood that one
who says 'Tom has a very good radio' is engaged on subversive
exercises against our pretty well-known and accepted standards in
the radio field is remote enough to be negligible. The fact that
sometimes it is hard to tell whether we have before us an X or a Y,
or something in between, is no reason on its own for doubting the
distinction between Xs and Ys; this holds when X = standard
setting and Y = standard using.

The suggestion that I now wish to make is that (at least so far
as the first pattern of analysis is concerned) Stevenson fails satis-
factorily to recognise and accommodate this distinction between
standard setting and making standard-using evaluative judgements.
In what situation would the utterance 'I approve of this, please do
so as well' in fact seem to be in place? The best suggestion I can
make is that we imagine ourselves at a very early stage of standard
setting, perhaps with reference to a newly invented kind of musical
instrument of which the most desirable tone colour, etc., has not
yet been settled. Perhaps one of us, after experimenting with a few
samples will finally say, holding up a sample, 'Well, can't we all

agree to approve of this one?'. This will be a useful move since, if we can agree on it, we shall have begun to achieve some standards; we can analyse how this instrument differs from those we can agree not to approve of. Thus Stevenson's 'I approve of this, please do so as well' seems to be nearer to a standard setting 'Can't we agree to count this as good' than to 'This is good'. In attempting to get the appeal for the standard-setting agreement accepted it may well be that it will be proper to mention any fact which is thought likely to influence others to accept the proposal, so far as we are merely concerned with logical propriety. It is, indeed, open to anyone to put forward his suggestions as to what the standards should be, when we are at the standard-setting stage or considering a reform of standards, without any possibility of his being mistaken. If this is to be called relativism, then at this point relativism is perhaps correct.

But, failing to observe the distinction between setting standards and making evaluations based on standards already set, Stevenson offers the first pattern of analysis as an acceptable picture of the judgement 'This is good', which would normally be a standard-using evaluation. It is the kind of judgement that might be made by a judge at a show, by a husband of his wife's cooking, or by an examiner of an examination paper. Yet on such occasions we are not attempting by persuasion to secure agreement to a standard of evaluation; we are presuming agreed standards to express an inter-subjectively acceptable attitude to something. If the judgement is not acceptable there must have been some error—the judge will not be invited to judge the cheese at next year's show. Of course there will be marginal cases which will be subjective, if that is the word, in the way that all judgements, evaluative or otherwise, are subjective in marginal cases; there are also fields where the standards are too loose, too obscure or too tentative for it to be appropriate to speak of anything so definite as a mistake. But though it is idle to ask whether Bach or Beethoven is the better composer, and a matter of opinion whether Double Gloucester is a better cheese than Leicester, it is obvious that both Bach and Beethoven are better composers than I am and that both cheeses are better than common mouse-trap. On the ordinary occasions of life to tell somebody that something is good is not to attempt to secure agreement in attitude but to supply a useful piece of information.

Further, the distinction between setting and using standards has consequences concerning the question whether we can speak of valid and invalid arguments for evaluations. Where there are no standards of merit it is no doubt idle to distinguish between valid and invalid grounds for a preference. But when we are using standards, which have been agreed as a result of the success of standard-setting proposals, the case is different. Though reference to other facts, securing agreement of belief on other matters, is not debarred, there is a peculiar relevance which some facts have, namely, the facts which show that the agreed standards are in fact attained by the thing which is being claimed to be good. Thus, if you are selling me cheese and have claimed that it is good cheese, there is nothing reprehensible in your pointing out to me that the Duke of London always eats that cheese; if I believe the Duke to be a discerning person I may well be influenced by this fact. But, except in the unlikely event that being eaten by the Duke is an accepted standard for cheese, it will not be relevant in the way that butter-fat content, texture, taste and the like are relevant. Schematically, if ABCD are the standards of merit in Xs, then it is specially relevant to mention that a specimen of X is A or B or C or D in proof that it is good. Further, 'This is ABCD, therefore it is good' is a valid argument, whereas 'It is the Duke of London's birthday, therefore this is good' is not merely ineffective but invalid; however, more will be said later about validity. It would be a mistake to suggest that all attempts to secure acceptance of an evaluative judgement by what, if construed as an argument, would be an invalid one are equally objectionable. It may well be that at times persuasion will be justified where argument fails or would be ineffective; but the distinction between valid argument and effective persuasion remains intact.

It is surely obvious that there would be no point in making standard-setting proposals if we did not envisage subsequent use of the standards. We do not wish to secure this agreement merely for the sake of a cosy agreement in attitude. Once we have secured agreement on standards, if and when we can, they are of great utility. Given common honesty, business men can now act on suppliers' value judgements of goods without invariable and detailed inspection. Buyers of rare gramophone records regularly trust to the judgement of the physical condition of the records given in the catalogues (indicated by the letters M, E, etc.) and find the system satisfactory; and we can order perishable vegetables from a reliable firm by telephone: 'Are the lettuces good today?—Not quite at their best, ma'am.' It is greed and dishonesty which set limits to our ordinary daily acceptance of value judgements as information, not relativity.

We have allowed, as a logical truism, that until standards have been set there can be no distinction between sound and unsound reasons for evaluation or preference. We have, as yet, not contested the suggestion that at the stage of standard-setting there are no good reasons for having some standards rather than others, that this is an area in which psychologically effective persuasion is our sole resource. But this does not follow from the logical truism, and we shall examine it later when we are armed with more effective intellectual tools.

At the beginning of this section of the discussion four contentions of Stevenson were listed as erroneous. The suggestion was made that each of these errors stemmed from a failure to observe the distinction between setting and using standards. We shall now go once more through the four points in recapitulatory justification of this suggestion.

(1) 'When someone says that something is good he does no more than to express his own personal approval in words which are also calculated to arouse the approval of his hearers.' This is an appropriate, though inadequate, model of standard-setting but not of standard-using; it is more relevant to 'Let us count things like this as good' than to 'This is good'.

(2) 'There is no logical reason of any kind why agreement on facts should secure agreement in attitude.' This is true at the stage

of setting standards. But given agreed standards it is irrational to admit the standards to be satisfied but to refuse to admit that the thing is good.

(3) 'No fact is logically more relevant to a disagreement in attitude than any other fact.' Possibly this is true while standards are still being set or do not exist at all. But when standards are agreed on, the fact that the object in question does or does not fulfil some standard has got a special relevance.

(4) 'There can be no distinction between valid and invalid arguments from facts to evaluations.' Though this may, so far as we have gone, be true of arguments in favour of standard-setting proposals, it is surely false of arguments making use of existing standards.

Thus we find that on each point what Stevenson holds has a higher plausibility if we take him to be referring only to standard-setting proposals. But in fact he surely wishes to claim that what he says has relevance to ordinary evaluative judgements, neglecting the fact that these can regularly be checked by reference to standards.

This criticism is not final. When we have taken note of the second pattern of analysis, which we shall immediately do, we shall have to show, if we can, that all the criticisms apply *mutatis mutandis* to this pattern of analysis also. But next time our argument can be briefer.

6

STEVENSON'S ETHICS AND LANGUAGE

(concluded)

The second pattern of analysis

It might well be held that our criticism of Stevenson on the basis of his first pattern of analysis alone has been premature. For his claim is that evaluations are *sui generis*, and therefore to be adequately analysed in no way which does not incorporate their distinctive feature—language used emotively. But he thinks that we can to some extent overcome this difficulty by offering two different patterns of analysis which will distort the original in rather different ways, so that by giving due heed to both we may get a reasonably adequate composite picture. We must now turn, therefore, to the second pattern of analysis, admitting that all our criticism so far must be regarded as provisional.

Stevenson first adumbrates the second pattern in Section 3 of the fourth chapter of his book. It is, in outline, as follows. When we say 'This is good' of a particular kind of thing, certain descriptions of the thing are normally suggested by such a judgement. Stevenson gives the example that when a clergyman says of a girl that she is good it suggests that she is chaste, kind and pious. He then says that on the *first* pattern of analysis we regard a statement of one's own approval and an evocation of approval in others (I approve of this—please do so as well) as being the *meaning* of the judgement, while the description of the object (chaste, kind and pious, for example) is regarded as merely *suggested*. On the second pattern the description is regarded as the meaning of the judgement and the approval as merely suggested. He does things this way because, in his opinion, it is impossible to decide in the case of a vague word like 'good' whether we should regard the approval as meant and the description as suggested, or *vice versa*. This interpretation of Stevenson's views is amply confirmed by the general account of the second pattern of analysis in the first paragraph of chapter IX of *Ethics and Language*, and by the schema of the second pattern which immediately follows (p. 207):

'This is good' has the meaning of 'This has qualities or relations X, Y, Z, . . .', except that 'good' has as well a laudatory emotive meaning which permits it to express the speaker's approval, and tends to evoke the approval of the hearer.

Note that on this account 'This is good' actually has the descriptive meaning 'This has the qualities X, Y, Z, . . .', apart from emotive meaning. For example, 'Mary is good', when said by a clergyman, will perhaps have the descriptive meaning 'Mary is chaste, kind and pious' to use Stevenson's own example. But this example is perhaps not altogether satisfactory, for it is reasonable to suppose that all these epithets, 'chaste', 'kind' and 'pious', are themselves to a greater or lesser degree evaluative; it would be better to have an example where the descriptive meaning is sternly non-evaluative. Let us suppose that on the second pattern of analysis 'This is a good tyre' will have some such descriptive meaning as 'This tyre lasts longer than most tyres, makes less noise than most tyres, and requires an unusually high lateral force to make it skid'.

Thus, in so far as it is not emotive, 'This is good' will be an empirical statement according to both patterns of analysis. But whereas on the first pattern the (allegedly) empirical component was 'I approve', now the empirical meaning is a description of *this*. 'This is good' will presuppose that, by definition, 'good' means 'X, Y, Z, . . .' in this sort of context, but it will not be itself an (ordinary) definition. It will use the definition in order to make the statement 'This is X, Y, Z, . . .' in an abbreviated form, and at the same time, via the emotive meaning of 'good', to express and evoke approval.

The sort of definition which is implied, according to Stevenson, by the use of 'good' as equivalent to the description 'X, Y, Z, ...' is called by him a persuasive definition; it is called a persuasive definition in that it is a device which is used in order to get X, Y, Z things approved of. He gave an excellent general account of persuasive definitions in an article in *Mind* in 1938, and provided many interesting examples of their use in both the article and *Ethics and Language*. None of the criticism that will shortly be offered here should obscure the general merit of this idea of Stevenson's; that we do make use of, say, the favourable aura of the term 'democracy' to define democracy in a way which makes our preferred form of government a paradigm of democracy is quite undeniable.

Stevenson insists that the second pattern of analysis is essentially equivalent to the first. We can analyse 'This is a good tyre' either according to the first pattern, where 'This tyre is long-wearing, noiseless and skid-proof' is treated as a supporting description used to gain agreement to the evaluative judgement which consists in the statement and evocation of approval, or according to the second pattern, where the judgement is treated as equivalent to the description, the expression and evocation of approval being taken as implied or suggested. On the first pattern disagreement in attitude will be displayed in the form 'Are being long-wearing, noiseless and skid-proof good reasons for approval of the tyre?'; on the second pattern disagreement in attitude will be displayed in the form 'Is being long-wearing, noiseless and skid-proof a satisfactory definition of a good tyre?'. But the disagreement will be essentially the same on both occasions. So we find, if Stevenson is right, that the second pattern raises no new considerations about the questions of the objectivity, relativity, and the like of evaluations, as he himself says; it will merely provide a new way of raising the same issues. The claim is that, because of its vagueness, 'This is good' can be treated with equal justice as having either of the two forms.

It is unnecessary to offer further detailed exposition, for we have before us a clear and internally consistent view, which must now be subjected to critical examination. The first question to be raised is whether we ever take 'good' to be identical in meaning with 'XYZ', where X, Y and Z are natural characters and relations, so that the question whether something is XYZ is in itself one involving only belief and not attitude. It will be assumed that the stock criticisms of naturalism are not relevant in the light of Stevenson's general view.

But before embarking on this question a preliminary distinction between vagueness and ambiguity must be made. A word is vague when on certain marginal occasions there is no way of determining whether the word can be correctly applied or not. Thus, to use the well-worn example, 'bald' is vague because, though it is often clear beyond dispute that a man is or is not bald, it is easy to find a head of which it cannot be said with security either that it is or that it is not bald; to say either will cause uneasy misgivings. The essential feature of a vague word is that the boundaries of its correct use are fuzzy like the edge of a shadow on rough ground.

Ambiguity is a very different thing from vagueness. 'Vague' is opposed to 'precise', 'ambiguous' to 'unambiguous' or 'univocal'. A vague but unambiguous word has fuzzy boundaries to the one area of its proper use whereas an ambiguous but precise word has two or more sharply defined areas of use. We can illustrate the point diagrammatically thus:

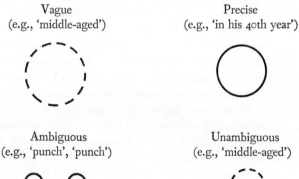

Other examples of ambiguous words are 'bat' (implement or animal) and 'bowl' (implement and action). It is clearly possible for a word to be ambiguous and also vague in one or more of its meanings.

We may now apply this distinction to the question raised. Stevenson repeatedly says that it is possible to make persuasive definitions of 'good' because it is a vague word. Thus he says (op. cit., p. 207): 'What sort of definitions may be instances of the second pattern? . . . It will not do to admit of any substitutions whatsoever. If that were done "good" would be a possible synonym for any term in the language which has both a laudatory and a descriptive meaning; and though "good" is vague, it is not so vague as that.' On the next page he adds: 'it may be observed that the boundaries for the "natural" meanings that may be ascribed to "good", as is true of any vague term, are so shadowy and unstable that it is difficult to specify them even in a rough way'. Now it may well be true that 'good' is a vague word, but what Stevenson in fact ascribes to it is ambiguity and, indeed, a double dose of ambiguity.

The first dose of ambiguity is administered as follows. It is quite clear that the descriptive meaning that can plausibly be ascribed to 'good' will have to vary enormously according to the kind of thing under consideration. Stevenson has suggested that the descriptive meaning that might be attached by a clergyman to 'good' when used of a girl is 'chaste, kind, and pious'; we have offered the not unplausible example of 'good' meaning 'noiseless, skid-proof and long-wearing' when applied to tyres. Now it is possible that we might wish girls to be noiseless, but we could hardly require them to be skid-proof or long-wearing except in a transferred or meta-phorical sense; nor should we readily understand one who said that by a good tyre he meant a tyre that was chaste, kind and pious. Thus Stevenson must ascribe two totally different meanings to 'good' when used of girls and tyres. Further totally different senses of 'good' would have to be invoked as we applied the word to apples, cabbages, holidays and so on. Thus, not allowing at all for any disagreement about or ambiguity in the descriptive meaning of 'good' as applied to any one kind of thing, 'good' will have to have, on Stevenson's view, as many different punning meanings as there are kinds of things to which it is applied. A conscientious lexicographer would need to allot about twenty volumes of his dictionary to the letter G. So clearly here what is alleged is ambiguity of fantastic proliferation, not a bit of fuzziness at the edges.

But this is surely all wrong. We may take an analogy from nonevaluative language to explain what has happened. If I say that a table is high and that a mountain is high, it would be queer to say that I have used the word 'high' ambiguously. Certainly if I say that a table is high you will expect its top to be of the order of four feet from the ground, and if I say that a mountain is high you will expect its top to be some thousands of feet above sea level. But 'high' does not *mean* 'over four feet' when used of tables and 'several thousand feet' when used of mountains. We mean the same in both cases (presumably something like 'more prominent than most of its kind'), and use being over four feet or over several thousand feet as a standard in the different cases. It seems that Stevenson is making a mistake about 'good' analogous to that which would be made by saying that 'high' had as many different punning meanings as the variety of things to which it applied. He treats the various criteria or standards for deciding whether members of different classes of things are good as what we mean by calling them good, which is analogous to treating the criteria for a mountain's being high as what we mean by calling it high. Part of the enormity of this is concealed by talking of vagueness rather than ambiguity, though ambiguity is the right word for the state of affairs alleged by Stevenson.

So much for the first dose of ambiguity which Stevenson injects into our use of the apparently simple word 'good'; we must now isolate the second. If a word, like 'bald', is vague, then we cannot be certain ourselves or hope to secure agreement in marginal cases; but we can easily secure agreement in all but marginal cases. If a man has at most a few short hairs round the back of his neck then all, clergy and freethinkers, will agree that he is bald, and manifestly most schoolboys are not bald. But there will be cases when I will refer to somebody as bald and you will protest that you would not count *him* as bald; sometimes, though not in this case, it will be important to secure agreement in a marginal case, as when it is a question whether somebody was driving *carelessly*. Now Stevenson sometimes speaks as though he wanted to maintain that things were like this in regard to the goodness of any one kind of thing, as when he says in a passage already quoted that 'The boundaries for the "natural" meanings that may be ascribed to "good", as is true of any vague term, are so shadowy and unstable that it is difficult to specify them even in a rough way.' But is this really his view? Does he think that all will agree with the clergyman that a girl is good if she is preeminently chaste, kind and pious, but there might be some dispute in a marginal case, when the girl is only conventionally pious and only fairly kind? Clearly he does not. Does he even mean that there will be some slight ambiguity in the meaning of 'good' when applied to girls, resulting from its vagueness, so that some will mean, say, 'chaste, kind and pious', others 'chaste, kind and devout', others 'chaste, kind, truthful and pious' and so on? Once again, he clearly does not mean this, for he is envisaging the possibility that chastity and piety do not matter so long as the girl is kind, honest, sincere and loyal. But this raises a strong likelihood that what one man, the cleric, will count as a *central* case of goodness will be wholly rejected by another, or that the cleric will regard as beyond redemption one admired by the other. If this is either vagueness or ambiguity it must clearly be regarded as the latter. So the double dose of ambiguity which must be ascribed to 'good' on Stevenson's view has now been described; firstly the ambiguity of 'good' when used of different kinds of things in a single person's vocabulary, and secondly the ambiguity of 'good' when applied to the same thing by persons who differ markedly in attitude.

I do not in fact wish to claim that 'good' is ambiguous, but only that Stevenson's account makes it ambiguous rather than vague. I should wish to deny that the descriptive 'XYZ' should be regarded as the meaning of 'good'. One way in which Stevenson is led to the opposite view seems to be this. He thinks it is supported by such perfectly good English sentences as 'By a "good" college president I mean one who is an industrious executive . . .' (op. cit. p. 208). This use of 'mean' is indeed standard; here are other examples of it: 'By a square meal I mean roast beef and Yorkshire pudding', 'By a funny hat I mean one like Mrs Moon's', 'By clever I meant cleverer than you'. But nobody is going to claim that 'square' sometimes means 'consisting of roast beef and Yorkshire pudding' or that 'funny' sometimes means 'like Mrs Moon's' and the like. I might say that by a good holiday I mean one in an area of Southern France unfrequented by British and Americans; would Stevenson or anybody else wish to say that I think that I have given one, no doubt rare, meaning which the word 'good' may bear? In fact we use the expression 'I mean' in a wide variety of ways, and it is not to be assumed that we can treat 'By X I mean Y' as equivalent to 'I take X to mean the same as Y'.

So our first criticism of the second pattern of analysis has been that while ostensibly relying on a reasonable claim to some vagueness in the word 'good' in marginal cases, it in fact invokes an incredible double dose of ambiguity. The second criticism is a repetition, *mutatis mutandis*, of one made of the first pattern— that it is a fair schematic representation of standard-setting situations, but leaves no room for the using of standards once they have been set. Part of our first criticism of the second pattern could be expressed by saying that it treats standard-setting as a case of persuasive definition, thereby confusing criteria of evaluation with the meaning of evaluative terms; now we must add that even so standard-setting has its point only as a preliminary to standard-using. But our present criticism is quite independent of the other for its force; if we stick to the language of definition and meaning we can say that definition, even when persuasive, is only a preliminary to the use of the terms defined.

Certainly, when setting up standards where none yet exist, or when attempting to modify existing ones, I may say 'An X should count as good only if it is ABC'. That is no doubt persuasion, though not, I should say, a matter of definition but of standard setting. But surely sometimes all but a few cranks get persuaded to employ ABC as the standards or criteria for the merit of Xs. We can now no longer persuade people about Xs, because they are already persuaded. What we can now do is to use the agreement gained; we can evaluate Xs on the agreed inter-subjective basis of the accepted criteria ABC. Now when we say 'This is a good X because it is ABC' there will be no persuasive element in our judgement, which does not stop it from being an evaluation, and perhaps a useful one.

I need not elaborate this criticism, for it is plainly the same as that made of the first pattern of analysis. There 'This is good' is treated as stating the speaker's attitude and trying to get others to share this attitude to the kind of thing in question. Our criticism of this was, in brief, that it seems to be an elucidation of 'Let's count this as good' rather than of 'This is good' and thus fails to allow that the point of persuading people to common attitudes is that we can then evaluate things on the basis of a shared attitude. In the second pattern 'This is good' is treated as saying 'Count the characteristics ABC which this has as what we mean by calling it good', and here the criticism is again that this is at best an account of the standard-setting 'Count Xs as good on standards ABC' and thus neglects the point that the reason for getting people to accept standards, of persuading them to adopt them, is that we may afterwards make use of the standards thus agreed on.

This section may appropriately end with one final analogy. Suppose that I were to say 'Count the true colour of a thing as being the way it looks in clear daylight'; here I should be trying to persuade you to adopt clear daylight as the standard situation for determining the true colours of things. Now let us suppose that you all agree to do this; we can now go on to settle definitely disputes about the colour of a piece of cloth and also to give each other dependable information about the colour of things. But there would be no point at all in getting you to agree to count the true colour of things as their colour in clear daylight unless I had in mind the use in this kind of way of the agreement gained. Perhaps someone will come along who uses the appearance in pure white light or even in red light as the criterion of true colour; we shall then be reduced to confusion unless we ignore him, or adopt his criterion of white light, which he might persuade us to do by showing that it provides still finer and easier discrimination of shades (if it does). But it is very desirable to have some criterion of true colour; the mere fact that something sometimes looked grey, for example, would be of little use if I wished to make a purchase by mail order. We must have inter-subjective standards. The problem of gaining and the reasons for requiring agreed standards of goodness seem to me to be parallel to this analogue.

7

VALIDITY

We have seen that Stevenson and the other emotive theorists regard an ethical or other evaluative judgement as being essentially the response of the agent to a feeling or attitude and a means of stimulating similar feelings and attitudes in others. Consequently anything brought forward in support of such a judgement has to be interpreted as a reinforcement of such a stimulus, causally rather than logically related to the judgement. It is clear that on such a view there can be no distinction between valid and invalid arguments to evaluative conclusions, and Stevenson expressly denies that such a distinction can be made. He does not, however, assert this merely as a consequence of his theory, but produces a specific argument against the distinction in ethical contexts which should be examined.

In chapter VII of *Ethics and Language* the argument proceeds much as follows:

Premiss (*a*): The only way in which we can ask whether an ethical statement is true is by asking whether the speaker does actually approve of what he evaluates favourably.

Premiss (*b*): But when we argue ethical questions we are not arguing this sort of question.

Conclusion from (*a*) *and* (*b*): Therefore in ethical argument we are not raising questions of truth.

Premiss (*c*): But the notion of validity is wrapped up with the notion of truth—a valid argument is one which gives true conclusions from true premisses.

Final Conclusions: Therefore the question of validity does not arise in arguments to ethical conclusions.

This argument, given the safeguards and qualifications which Stevenson inserts, is undoubtedly valid; the conclusion follows from the premisses. But are the premisses true?

There can be no doubt that the first premiss is true according to Stevenson's first pattern of analysis, which treats an evaluation as in part a declarative, autobiographical statement about the speaker's attitudes and emotions combined with an emotive appeal to others to feel likewise. We have already given reasons for finding this analysis wholly unacceptable. But we cannot lightly dismiss this premiss as being dictated by the first pattern of analysis, for other philosophers with a serious interest in ethics have denied that ethical judgements are true or false without making any such analysis. Thus Margaret Macdonald, in her article 'Ethics and the Ceremonial Use of Language' in *Philosophical Analysis* (Ed. Black, Cornell, 1950), says that in non-ethical fields 'Is *p*?' and 'Is *p* true?' are usually equivalent and then continues as follows: 'It is ... sensible to ask "Is murder wrong?" Now, however, the parallel seems to fail. For it does not seem equally sensible to ask "Is it true that murder is wrong?" or "Is it true that he ought not to have been murdered?" These forms are quite unnatural and, I suggest, would puzzle the plain man. For he does not use them'. Miss Macdonald continues by saying that the same conclusion would be reached if we took examples involving more contentious moral issues, and gives some. Here then, and it is not an isolated case, we find Stevenson being supported by another philosopher on grounds of actual use and not of theory.

Now I have no doubt at all that Miss Macdonald is right in thinking that we should all find something odd, at least in ordinary contexts, in ethical questions formulated in the 'Is it true that ... ?' idiom. Like her, I might ask whether killing was wrong, but not whether it is true that killing is wrong. But is the explanation the

one that she offers, that ethical judgements are not true or false?
In fact it seems that in non-evaluative contexts also, where truth
and falsity clearly arise, it would usually be as odd to use the 'Is it
true that . . . ?' formula as in evaluative contexts. The point which
Miss Macdonald notices only as a feature of ethical discourse is in
fact a feature of all discourse. Thus in most contexts it would be
very queer to ask the time by saying 'Is it true that it is 6 p.m.
yet?' instead of 'Is it 6 p.m. yet?' We should raise the question that
way only if someone had asserted that it was 6 p.m. already and
we wished to query the assertion. Similarly, when serving at the
meal table I should ask you 'Do you like rice pudding?' rather
than 'Is it true that you like rice pudding?', a formula which, once
again, would be reserved for the expression of incredulous surprise
or the like. Again, if I had heard casually that your friend Jones
was sick, I might ask you as an authority: 'Is it true that Jones is
sick?'; but if Jones, whom we both know equally well, is behaving
rather oddly and neither of us is a medical authority, I should ask
'Is he ill, perhaps?', in a meditative way, not 'Is it true that he is
ill?'.

Thus the use of the 'Is it true that . . . ' formula seems to be
typically in contexts where one appeals to somebody as an authority
to settle an issue already raised. But ethical issues rarely arise in
which it would be sensible to treat somebody else as an authority;
we normally raise questions like 'Is killing (adultery, drug-taking)
wrong?' in the meditative way that invites co-operation rather than
appeals to authority. But when an assertion is made in the evaluative
field that we find surprising or otherwise unacceptable, and when
it is of the special kind on which there can be authorities, it does
not seem at all odd to ask 'Is it true?'. Thus if it be asserted that
people are not as morally upright nowadays as they were in
Victorian times, and you happen to be very old indeed and a
person whose judgement I respect, I might well ask you 'Is it true
that people are not as good nowadays as in Victorian times?'. No
doubt I am in this example treating you as a factual rather than a
moral authority; but I should not treat anybody as a purely moral
authority. If I thought that some class of persons were moral

authorities I do not think that there would be any oddity in my going to one of them on a contentious issue and asking 'Father, is it true that theatre-going is dissolute, as I have heard say?'. But, in any case, the question asked in the example about the Victorians is a moral one and is natural, which is all that I need to claim. So to Miss Macdonald, Stevenson and others who take the same line, I should answer that it is possible to raise moral issues by means of the 'Is it true that . . . ?' formula, and that the comparative rarity of the formula is to be explained by the fact that there are not in general moral authorities rather than by the irrelevance of truth and falsity to moral issues. But if I do ask you about the comparative merits of Victorians and moderns, it is a genuine question about which I can seek the truth; did the Victorians approach more nearly than we do to the moral standards which we recognise or did they not? Either they did or they did not, and one of these will be the true answer. Thus it is not lack of subject matter, but lack of authorities that leads us to raise rather than ask others for answers to moral issues; and when we raise questions we do not employ the 'Is it true that . . . ?' formula, whether the subject under discussion is moral or of any other character.

We cannot therefore accept premiss (a). But we can surely accept premiss (b), that when we argue about morality we are not arguing the question whether the speaker does or does not have the attitudes which he says he has. I however accept this premiss because I deny that there is any autobiographical element in ethical judgements of the type under discussion, not because, like Stevenson, I regard this element as present, but not the one which is challenged.

Premiss (c) is to the effect that the notion of validity is wrapped up with the notion of truth. Stevenson certainly wishes to claim this. Thus he says (op. cit., p. 154) that 'no matter how else we may define "valid" we shall very likely want to retain a sense which is intimately related to "true" '. I should again find this view surprising if it were not so common. But we speak of valid driving licences, valid forms of marriage, valid contracts, valid orders and the like, where there seems to be no intimate connexion with questions of truth. What truth, except that it is valid, follows from the fact that my driving licence is valid for three years? The criterion of the validity of an argument may well be that if its premises are true its conclusion must be true; but this no more shows that the notion of validity has to be explained in terms of truth than the fact that a criterion of a valid marriage is that both parties must be without an existing spouse shows that the notion of validity has to be defined in terms of the concept of spinsterhood. It is indeed much more plausible to hold that the notion of argument is bound up with the notion of validity and invalidity; it might well be thought to be analytic that every argument is either valid or invalid, somewhat as it is analytic that every statement is true or false—in fact I am more certain of the former of these two than of the latter.

So it seems to me that the true conclusion on this point is that Stevenson is wrong in attempting to distinguish, on his premises, between argument and other forms of persuasion. If what he calls argument cannot be valid or invalid, it would be better if he merely recognised two forms of persuasion, one which invokes statements of fact and one which does not. This would not involve any abuse of the concept of argument. It seems that Stevenson lulls us into a false sense of familiarity and security when he allows that there can be argument about evaluative issues, since he goes on to deny that there is any distinction between valid and invalid ethical arguments.

We are not now in a position to embark on a full independent discussion of the validity and invalidity of ethical argument. We have not surveyed anywhere near a wide enough field of evaluative argument for that. But surely we have got a sufficient, if not a necessary, criterion of the validity of an argument from facts to an evaluation of the type 'This is a good X'; the criterion is that the fact adduced should be the fact that the thing in question has the various characteristics which are the accepted criteria of merit for the kind of thing in question. If we compare the argument 'Mr Justice Blackstone is a good judge because he is impartial' with the 'argument' 'Mr Justice Blackstone is a good judge because he was born on the ninth day of August', it is very unplausible to regard the two as differing only in psychological effectiveness.

Impartiality is, date of birth is not, a criterion of merit in judges.

It may certainly be urged that if we are to have a valid argument we must bring in the criteria of merit as a separate premiss thus:

> ABC are the criteria of merit for Xs
> But this X is ABC
> Therefore this is a good X

This is unobjectionable, but it is not necessary. It is always an open matter what one brings into an argument as premisses; when the criteria are well known and undisputed there is no reason why we should not treat them rather as principles of the argument. We could compare the question whether 'Tom is a grocer; therefore he is a tradesman' is a valid argument or whether there is a suppressed premiss that all grocers are tradesmen.

In conclusion to this discussion of validity, I should say that it is much more plausible to suppose that the emotive theory is mistaken than that we are always in error when we call an ethical judgement true or an ethical argument valid. Stevenson had the great merit of being the first modern empiricist in the Anglo-Saxon tradition to take the problems of evaluation seriously; his views were suggestive of much, in itself better, that was to follow. Indeed the line of criticism that we are now pursuing would have been unthinkable prior to his work, and nobody should confuse persistent criticism with denigration.

8

THE VOCABULARY OF EVALUATION

The vocabulary of words which find their characteristic use in evaluative and normative contexts is very large. We shall later attempt to find some criterion of an evaluative term. So far we have examined the views of the emotivists only about the use of 'good' and 'approve'; but there are many terms in addition to these that their theory purports to cover:—ought, right, duty, beautiful, excellent, pretty, charming, etc., etc. We must now examine what they have to say about these terms, or some of them. Also it is clear that many evaluative terms, 'good' for example, can be used in many contexts which are not ethical; we speak of good arguments, apples, pictures, economic policies and a whole host of other kinds of things. It will be as well to consider what the emotivists have to say about this fact. As a warning of what is to come I now predict that we shall find them very unsatisfactory both on the question of the different kinds of evaluative term and on the question of the varied uses of particular value terms, and we shall be led into a long, but not, I hope, uninteresting discussion on these points.

It will be a fair generalisation from which to start that the emotivists did not treat these two questions as distinct, but that the answer that they would give to them is plain. Words, they held, which have an emotive meaning differ from each other only in descriptive meaning (if any) and the particular strength and flavour of emotion that they expressed and evoked. A few quotations will quickly substantiate this interpretation. Stevenson says (*Mind*, 1937, p. 24): 'Let us now apply these remarks in defining "good". This word may be used morally or non-morally. I shall deal with the non-moral usage almost entirely, but only because it is simpler. The main points of the analysis will apply equally well to either usage.' On the same point he says on page 90 of *Ethics and Language*: 'We may recognise a sense where "good" abbreviates "morally good", and refers not to *any* kind of favour that the speaker has, but only to the kind that is marked by a special serious-ness or urgency. And we may recognise another sense, similar to that of "swell" or "nice", which refers descriptively to attitudes of the common-garden variety.' On page 97 of the same work he speaks of the other question of the relation of 'good' to other evaluative terms as follows:

Certain theorists are accustomed to make a sharp distinction between 'good' and 'right', as though the terms involved quite disparate problems of analysis. The present writer can find little ground for such a distinc-tion, either in common usage or elsewhere. There are slight emotive differences, and different ranges of ambiguity for the more specific senses; but that is true of any pair of ethical terms. Only one point of difference is conspicuous, and that is not at all profound. Note that it is quite idiomatic to say, 'He is a good man', or 'That is a good book', but not at all idiomatic to say 'He is a right man', or 'That is a right book'. Thus 'right' is much less suited than 'good' for judging *persons* or *things*; and a moment's consideration will show that it is usually reserved for judging people's *actions*. It is quite idiomatic to say 'His philanthropic action was morally right'. Now it is difficult to believe that this is any-thing more than a linguistic nicety, together with a means of giving the adjective 'right', by a limitation of the substantives it can modify, an emotive meaning that makes it influence actions more specifically and directly. In other respects 'right' acts like 'good' (for the first-pattern type of analysis) in indicating the speaker's favourable attitude, and influencing that of the hearer.

Stevenson sees that one cannot completely equate 'right' with 'duty' and 'obligation', but again makes the difference one of emotive effect alone. He says (op. cit., p. 99): 'Evidently, "right" has a less coercive effect', and later (p. 100): 'The shade of menace that often attends "duty" and "ought" is the emotive, quasi-imperative counterpart of their use in indicating strong dis-approval of omission.' He is ready to acknowledge (op. cit., p. 101) that even the words 'duty', 'obligation' and 'ought' 'have in fact slightly different emotive colourings', but this is the only kind of difference that he allows. His views are fully set out in chapter IV, section 4, of *Ethics and Language*.

Ayer, in *Language, Truth and Logic*, had taken much the same line. Thus he says on page 113: 'Aesthetic terms are used in exactly the same way as ethical terms. Such aesthetic words as "beautiful" and "hideous" are employed, as ethical words are employed, not to make statements of fact, but simply to express certain feelings and evoke a certain response.' On page 108 he suggests that 'It is a duty to tell the truth' may have something of an imperative force in contrast to 'It is good to tell the truth', but does not follow this up to make it more than a matter of nuance of emotive force.

It is, then, a fair summary to say that the emotive theorists give a single account of all evaluative and normative terms, claiming that they differ from each other only in emotional nuance or purely idiomatic restrictions. In so far as they make an exception to this it is to allow to certain terms such as 'obligation' and 'duty' a 'coercive effect', 'a shade of menace', 'a quasi-imperative effect' (Stevenson), or 'the effect of commands' and a tendency to 'stimulate action' (Ayer).

But if a claim is made that 'ought' and 'duty', say, are essentially more concerned with evoking action, while 'good' has the function of evoking an attitude of approval, it is mistaken. We have already noted that to regard the expression of approval as the specific function fulfilled by judgements of goodness is erroneous; rather than that, we should say that it is one of the typical things that we do when we say that something is good. In some contexts ascription of goodness is quite directly concerned with action. Thus if a housewife complains that she simply cannot get her washing white and in response I say 'Well, you will find Bubblezone very good' I am recommending Bubblezone rather than expressing approval of it, as she after trying it may do. When I tell Mrs Scraggs that

Bubblezone is good it is a recommendation of a course of action, and I do not expect her to start to have an approving attitude to Bubblezone until she has tried it. So the use of 'good' can have a 'quasi-imperative effect' or a tendency to 'stimulate action'. On the other hand, while 'ought' and 'duty' are often used in guidance of action, this is a matter of context and not something essential. If I say to an old man 'He ought not to have married that gold-digger' what action am I attempting to stimulate? The third party has made his bed for better or worse and the old man is past following his example. I here hope at most to secure agreement to my attitude. Again, if the hero modestly says to the reporters who gather round him after he has been awarded his Victoria Cross 'I only did my duty' it is very doubtful whether he should be interpreted as stimulating those hard-bitten gentlemen to deeds of daring.

Thus, if the emotive theorists whose views we are now considering did wish to maintain that there was a difference of logical character between a set of words like 'good' which were concerned with arousing attitudes and another set including 'duty' and 'ought' which were specifically concerned with stimulating to action, they were surely mistaken. There is no such distinction of function. But I do not believe that they did make this mistake, for I doubt that they intended to claim that there was here a true difference of kind. I believe that they wished only to make a generalisation which they thought to be of interest but of no great theoretical importance. We shall therefore interpret them as holding that logically there is no difference between the character of various evaluative terms, or between the uses of these terms in various types of context, but only a slight difference in emotive colour and sometimes a subsidiary tendency to provoke action.

Let us consider whether this view is correct, starting with the first of the two questions that we distinguished. This is the question whether all the evaluative terms which the emotivists claimed to have characterised are in fact of one logical type. We shall start with a comparison and contrast of 'good' and 'right'. It will probably be agreed that if we detect any basic differences between 'right' and 'good' there is likely to be at least as great a difference between 'good' and 'duty' or 'good' and 'obligation'. But rightness and goodness will be taken as a test case.

The right and the good

We have seen that Stevenson, considering whether the terms 'right' and 'good' needed separate treatment, said that only one point of difference was conspicuous, a difference which could be dismissed as a mere linguistic nicety. This one point of difference was that we can speak of a good man or book, but not of a right man or book. We shall return later to this point, to consider for ourselves what significance it may have. Now let us consider what other conspicuous points of difference we can find between our use of 'right' and 'good'.

One very noticeable difference is that 'good' is what is sometimes called a scalar quality and 'right' is not. Crudely, we may say that adjectives which ascribe scalar qualities have comparatives and superlatives while those ascribing non-scalar qualities do not. To be good, worthy or admirable is to possess a scalar quality, since we can speak of the better, the best, the worthier, the worthiest, the more admirable and the most admirable. But this is a crude test; one modification that is required is that sometimes a scalar adjective has no grammatical comparative or superlative but is one of an ordered set of adjectives ascribing comparative merit, as A, B, C, D and E are scalar adjectives when used conventionally of examination papers and 'domestic', 'fancy', 'extra fancy' and 'super' are scalar adjectives when used of boxes of apples according to the conventions of the Ministry of Agriculture. Clearly the device of the ordered set permits far finer discrimination. But rightness is not scalar; we do not have the comparison 'right, righter, rightest', or 'right, more right, most right'. In this respect, perhaps significantly, 'proper' and 'legal' are like 'right'; there is not a properest course of action, nor can one action be more legal than another. When 'correct' is used as an approximate synonym of 'punctilious' or 'careful about protocol' it is scalar; we can say that somebody is the most correct hostess in London. But when 'correct' is used of answers to sums or to some particular act of placing guests in order of precedence it is not scalar; the answer to the sum is correct or incorrect. 'Five' is more nearly correct than 'Six' as an answer to 'What is two plus two?', but it is not more correct. Similarly, the guests are either in the correct places or they are not. Sometimes we find that the opposite of a non-scalar quality admits of degree; thus one action cannot be more right than another, but it is surely still more wrong to hit a benefactor over the head than merely to fail to show gratitude. But this is not always so. There are degrees neither of legality nor of illegality.

If we have already graded candidates in an examination, some as bad, others as poor, fair, good, very good and excellent, which is to place them on a scale of merit, we may or may not have to do something else, which is to decide which have passed and which have failed. The antitheses of right and wrong, legal and illegal, proper and improper, correct and incorrect (as used of answers to sums) are a matter of pass and fail. The comparisons of good, better and best, worthy, worthier and worthiest, fancy, extra-fancy and super are more like determining a class of honours. At Oxford the mark 'epsilon' (and at some American universities the mark E) has a special dual function, since it both indicates a degree of merit below delta (or D) and also that the candidate has failed. As a natural consequence there is some use for the more refined mark 'delta minus', but to add a minus sign to the epsilon would be a mere rhetorical flourish.

We can perhaps explain the difference between the scalar and the non-scalar, as found in the special discourse of evaluation, in some such way as this. When we use non-scalar adjectives like 'right', 'proper', 'legal' and 'correct' we are indicating that something is in accordance with some rule or set of rules, principles, specifications, instructions or similar requirements. What is not in accord with the rule is simply wrong, or incorrect, or illegal. But in the case of scalar qualities we are concerned with how near a thing comes to some ideal, how fully and how exactly it satisfies some set of standards. Since some of the standards will themselves be couched in terms of degrees of scalar natural properties (the rounder the better), and since it is possible that something will satisfy some of the standards but not others (a reliable but uncomfortable motor car) we are inevitably faced with judgements of degrees. If I tell you to get me a thing which is ABC, then you will have performed your task correctly, rightly, properly, if the thing you bring me has (in some degree) the characteristics A, B and C. But it may well be better, wiser, more helpful to bring me one which is very A, B and C than one which is only moderately so; and if you cannot correctly fulfil your task because there is nothing available which is ABC, it may still be better to bring one which is A and B, though not C, than one which has none of these features.

The matter may be presented schematically as follows: both goodness and rightness are determined by reference to other features which may themselves be scalar (fat, hot) or non-scalar (spherical, boiling). Questions of rightness are determined by whether all of some set of features are present, and, if the features are scalar, whether they are present at a certain degree, or within a certain range of degrees. Questions of goodness are determined by how many of some set of features are present, and if the features are scalar, how high a degree they reach. Clearly no such simple schema can be adequate to the facts.

It has traditionally been held, I think rightly, that different features are relevant to the rightness and to the goodness of a moral act. In utilitarian terms, motives determine the goodness of the act, consequences its rightness, and a similar distinction can easily be made in Kantian or intuitionist terms. I may do what all would agree was the right action in the circumstances from such a distorted motive that it is none the less a bad action, while a good, or even saintly, deed may turn out to be the wrong thing to do, perhaps because of unavoidable ignorance of fact. It is the temptation to seek martyrdom for the sake of reward in heaven that most worries Becket in Eliot's *Murder in the Cathedral* precisely because it is the greatest treason to do the right deed for the wrong reason. But, in the light of the distinctions which we have noted, it is important to see that it is not merely the case that different considerations are relevant to rightness and goodness but also that these considerations are relevant in different ways. For an action to be good it must answer more or less to certain criteria (no doubt connected with motives), and might have answered to these criteria in such a way as to have been still better or not quite as good. For an action to be right it must satisfy some definite requirements, in the simplest cases some elementary moral principle, so that if the requirements are satisfied the action is right and if not it is wrong.

The same difference in mode of relevance can be found elsewhere. Thus if a chess problem is set requiring mate in three moves my first move will be wrong if it leads to mate in four but not mate in three. But if I had made the same move in an actual game of chess then, though no doubt it would have been better to have made the move leading to mate in three as nearer to our ideals of elegance, there is no question at all of it being the wrong move or a wrong move. Moves in actual games are only wrong if they violate the rules of chess, and there is no rule that one must mate in the most economical way. Similarly in mathematics we distinguish between good, and even beautiful, proofs and correct proofs. A proof is correct if it does not violate the accepted principles of mathematics and good or beautiful if elegant, economical and the like. Elegance and economy are ideals of mathematics, not principles. But if you set me the problem of proving something without appeal to certain already proved theorems my solution will be wrong and not merely uneconomical if these theorems are in some way presupposed by it. By making it a rule that I must be economical in a certain way you have made economy an *ad hoc* principle of rightness.

Let us now return to the point noted by Stevenson, though rejected by him as without philosophical interest, that we cannot speak of a right man or a right book, as we can speak of a good man or book. But we can speak of the right man or book, as easily as of the good man or book. Moreover the right man or book may not be good. When the detective is looking for the murderer he has presumably only got the right man if he has got a bad man; if I ask for a thriller and you bring me Kant's *Critique of Pure Reason* I can say that you have not brought the right book without any adverse reflection on that great work. Moreover 'the worthy man' and 'the admirable man' are clearly near synonyms of 'the good man', while 'the correct man' and 'the proper man' are near synonyms of 'the right man'. Now we can speak of 'a proper man' or 'a correct man', though we would usually say 'a very proper man' or 'a very correct man'; but then 'correct' and 'proper' are being used as synonyms for 'punctilious about etiquette' and not at all as they are used when we speak of the detective catching the correct man or somebody being the proper man for the job.

The question which should now be asked is clear. When there is one man or book which some principles, rules, orders or instructions require us to select, choose, arrest or bring, we speak of this as the right man or book; why, if there is more than one man or book that may be selected in accordance with the instructions, should we not call each of these a right man or book? Clearly we could introduce this idiom into English in this way, but there are good reasons for not so doing. In the first place we already have such words as permissible and its synonyms to fulfil this task; a cricketer born in Yorkshire is an eligible man so far as the Yorkshire County Cricket Club are concerned; if there is nothing wrong with a book then it is a suitable or an unobjectionable book; pork is a legitimate food for Christians but not for Jews. Therefore we have no need for the introduction of the idom 'a right X'. In the second place it is positively undesirable to turn words with specific roles into undifferentiated synonyms; we do indeed show some tendency to weaken the word 'correct' by speaking of 'a correct answer' when more than one answer can be given, but a guardian angel usually prompts us to say rather 'a perfectly correct answer'. 'Perfectly correct' is, 'correct' is not, a synonym of 'permissible'.

So, to some extent I agree that it is a matter of idiom that we do not speak of a right man or book. But I do not find the point without philosophical interest. Certainly I should not agree that but for this idiomatic quirk we should have no means at all of distinguishing between the role of such words as 'right' and such as 'good'. Nor should this last sentence be taken to imply that I regard the differences between 'right', 'duty', 'ought' and 'obligation' to be trivial. They are not. But it is beyond our present scope to go into this question which Hart has begun to explore in his 'Natural rights' (*Phil. Review*, 1955) and 'Legal and moral obligation' (*Essays in Moral Philosophy*, Ed. Melden).

So far, then, from agreeing with the emotivists that there is little scope for philosophical discrimination between the various terms of evaluative and normative discourse, I think that this is a large and fruitful field for philosophical investigation, in which there is much still to be done.

D

9

GOOD OF A KIND AND GOOD
FROM A POINT OF VIEW

We have seen that the emotivists were wrong to try to give a single account of the uses of 'good' and 'right', or at least to claim that the terms differed only in the tinge of emotion involved, as is perhaps also the case with 'nice' and 'pleasant'. We now turn to the question whether they were right in trying to give a single account of the use of 'good' in all the types of context in which it occurs. In particular, we must enquire whether an account of its use with reference to apples, motor cars and cricketers can be regarded as applying without important modification to its use when applied to actions, men and motives in moral discourse. Is the only difference between judging that somebody is a good man and that something is a good cheese that we regard the former judgement as more important, solemn or urgent? For a long time I used to think that the emotivists were right about this, and published an article, 'On grading', in which I assumed that they were right about it. When I now attack this view I am, therefore, attacking what I now regard as my own former errors.

We have already, by criticism, suggested quite a number of alterations in the emotivists' view of our use of 'good'; I now summarily list a few of the most important:

(1) When in saying that something is good one somehow conveys that one approves of it, one is expressing one's approval, an essentially evaluative act, rather than making a declarative,

autobiographical statement about one's psychological condition.

(2) When we say that something is good the 'illocutionary force' of our utterance is as likely to be that of commendation, recommendation, praise or congratulation as expression of approval.

(3) We must recognise standard-using as well as standard-setting uses of 'good'. The natural description which Stevenson treats as being equated with goodness by a persuasive definition is, in standard-using situations, rather being assumed as an agreed standard for the evaluation of things of the kind in question.

So the alleged emotive force on the hearer of an evaluation— 'This is a good X'—is better regarded as an implied claim to his agreement to an evaluation on the basis of agreed standards. Moreover an evaluation made on the basis of such standards will be correct while one out of accord with these standards will be incorrect; as a corollary, an argument from the standards to an evaluation can be valid or invalid.

On the basis of these critical revisions, I should say that typically when we say 'This is a good X' we thereby commend, recommend, grade high, evaluate favourably (or something similar according to context) some given X among the things that are members of the class of Xs, are of the kind X, or fulfil the role of an X. I should further claim that we do this on the basis of some agreed criteria— the possession, or possession to an unusually high degree, of certain characteristics which are the standards for judging members of the class of Xs.

I have deliberately stated this view of the use of 'good' in this type of context vaguely and with alternative formulations, for we are not now concerned with trying to get the details right. I have no doubt that, if for 'X' we substitute 'apple' or 'motor car' or 'knife' or 'golfer' or 'secretary', or a host of other names of kinds of things (as an apple is a kind of thing) or roles (as being a golfer or secretary is a role that a person may fill), this view of our typical use of statements of goodness is substantially correct, even if in need of refinement. I shall now take the general correctness of this account for granted so far as many possible substitutions for 'X' are concerned, without worrying about the details. I can do this because the points I wish to make do not depend in any way upon such details. They must be allowed for in any account of goodness, however different from the one just sketched.

The first step in my argument will be to show that there are some possible substitutions for 'X' for which the above general account of judgements of the form 'This is a good X' is certainly incorrect.

If to say that something is a good X or is good as an X is to commend, express approval of, grade highly (or something of that sort) the thing in question as of the kind X or in the role of an X, there must clearly be some way of determining whether the thing is an X independently of determining whether it is a good one. If an explicit testing procedure would help, we may say that we must be able significantly to ask and answer the question 'Is this an X?' if we are to be able to ask and answer the question 'Is this good as a member of the kind of things called Xs?'. Clearly this can be done in the case of apples, motor cars and golfers; it is as proper to ask whether it or he is a good apple, motor car or golfer; the former question must be at least as easy to ask and answer as the latter. One could hardly be more certain that a thing was a good apple than that it was an apple.

But now consider the locution: 'This is a good thing from the farmers' point of view', said perhaps with reference to a piece of road construction or to a period of sunny weather. We should first notice that

A. This is a good road (period of weather) from the farmers' point of view is quite different from

B. This road (period of weather) is a good thing from the farmers' point of view.

It might well be doubted whether the example A is even an intelligible piece of English. It has no established use, but would presumably be the evaluation of something as of the kind road, though with restrictions. It would seem that anything said in support of it would have to refer to criteria which were criteria for the merits of roads, such as that its surface would bear caterpillar tractors without noticeable deterioration. To say that the road was good with the restriction 'from the farmers' point of view', instead of just saying that the road was a good one, would presumably serve principally to rule out as irrelevant such pros and cons as that it was or was not well-signposted to distant cities, a point of negligible importance to local farmers.

But the example B is quite different; the fact that something was a good road might indeed be a reason, among others, for saying that it was a good thing from the farmers' point of view. But this would not be so in the degenerate way in which the fact that something was a good road would be a reason for saying that it was a good road. This in itself shows that B must have a different sense from any that could be plausibly assigned to A. But further, it might be perfectly relevant to give reasons for saying of a road that it was a good thing from the farmers' point of view which had no relevance to the question whether it was a good road: for example, that it served as a barrier for agricultural land against flooding from some river. That a road serves as a barrier against flooding of adjacent land is no reason at all for saying that it is a good road, whether or not we add that the road is good from the farmers' point of view.

I shall take it then, as I believe is in any case obvious on the face of it, that B—'This road is a good thing from the farmers' point of view'—is not a paraphrase of A—'This is a good road from the farmers' point of view'. But 'This is a good thing from the farmers' point of view' is of the grammatical form 'This is a good X'. It is clear, however, that the question 'Is this a thing from the farmers' point of view?' is without sense; for nothing could count in favour of either an affirmative or a negative answer. We could of course sensibly raise the question whether this is a thing that it is wise, or prudent, or useful, to evaluate from the farmers' point of view. But that is quite another issue. One could also raise the question 'Is this a thing that is likely to affect farming interests?' significantly enough, but we do not use the question 'Is this a thing from the

D*

farmers' point of view?' in this way (or in any other) since we do not use it at all. Moreover, though we can say 'This is a good thing from the farmers' point of view', there would be something distinctly odd about 'This is a good thing likely to affect farmers' interests', which renders it implausible as a paraphrase. Again, parallel to 'This is a good thing from the farmers' point of view' we can say 'This is an indifferent thing from the farmers' point of view'; probably the President of the Farmers' Union would make some such response if officially consulted about regulations in the cotton spinning industry. But it is obviously absurd to say of anything that it is an indifferent thing likely to affect farming interests, since, if we were to use such a locution it could only be self-contradictory. It is quite clear that we cannot interpret 'thing from the farmers' point of view' as an alternative description of the class of things likely to affect farming interests.

If, then, there is no way of determining whether something is a 'thing from the farmers' point of view', we are justified in concluding that this expression does not name or otherwise designate a kind. From this it follows that when we say that something is a good thing from the farmers' point of view we are not judging it to be good of any kind, that we are not expressing approval of (recommending, commending) it as fulfilling the criteria of merit for any kind of thing. To controvert this conclusion it would have to be shown either that 'thing from the farmers' point of view' is the designation of a kind, which has just been disproved, or that whenever we say that something is good from the farmers' point of view we are covertly judging it to be good by the criteria appropriate to the members of some unmentioned kind. What this unmentioned kind would be is beyond my capacities of imagination.

So the first stage in my argument is now complete. It has been shown that there is at least one case in which we use a locution of the grammatical form 'This is a good X' in such a way that we are not evaluating a thing as good of a kind. The remaining two elements in the argument are, first, the contention that there are many other locutions of the grammatical form 'This is a good X' which, like 'This is a good thing from the farmers' point of view', are not used to evaluate something as good of a kind, and, secondly, an attempt to give a positive account which will cover at least some of these cases. I say 'at least some' because I have no wish to insist that we shall find an exhaustive dichotomy. It may well be that we sometimes use locutions of the form 'This is a good X' in ways unlike both 'good of the kind X' and 'good from the Y point of view'.

It might seem that of these two desiderata the instancing of other examples should come first. But anyone who accepts the one example given will not cavil at there being more and will readily think of them for himself; if he cannot, let him consider 'good thing from the butchers' ' (or 'the bakers' ' or 'the candle-stick makers' ') point of view. The interesting question is rather whether we can find further examples of greater philosophical interest, and before we embark on it we need to have before us a general positive description of the 'point of view' use of 'good', which I shall therefore attempt immediately.

Just as we can examine a person in a subject of his own choosing, so we can evaluate things in the role which they explicitly claim, or are claimed, to fill. We may evaluate a person who plays golf as a golfer or an object of a certain familiar shape and physical character as a spade. We can also evaluate things hypothetically in some role which they do not claim to fill, and perhaps have never attempted to fill; you could say of me that I would make a poor water-skier, or of a spade that it would make a poor cricket bat. We might even attempt to play cricket with a spade and conclude non-hypothetically that it does make a poor cricket bat. But there are limits to this; we could not say of a hurricane or of the Judicial Committee of the House of Lords that it makes a good, poor, or indifferent cricket bat, because, for different reasons, they could not (in the relevant sense of 'make') make cricket bats at all. A thing may, obviously, be good judged in one role and poor when judged in another. Sir Thomas Beecham is said to have said of a camel that made a mess on the stage at a performance of *Aida* which dissatisfied him that it was as an actor mediocre but as a critic superb.

But just as we may also examine people not in their special subject but in a general paper applicable to all, so we may also judge things not as being actually or potentially of some kind of fulfilling actually or potentially some role but from some general point of view, which might be affected by anything irrespective of its kind. Thus we might ask of someone who is a philosopher and might also become a water-skier, though a bad one, or of a spade, which might make at a pinch a very mediocre cricket bat, but which cannot become a cricket bat without ceasing to be a spade, whether he or it is a good thing from the farmers' point of view, though neither is a 'thing from the farmers' point of view' precisely because we are asking how they affect certain interests which anything that can affect any interest might conceivably affect. It is no doubt ridiculous in a way to ask of a philosopher or one particular spade whether he or it is a good thing from the farmers' point of view; but this is only a practical not a logical absurdity, which arises from the fact that both are manifestly of no significance at all from the farmers' point of view. But in saying this we are assessing them from the farmers' point of view. Surely it may be true and worth saying that Mussolini was a good thing from the Italian farmers' point of view, and a great soil scientist is a good thing from the farmers' point of view without any qualification.

I want, then, to contrast being good from a point of view, of which I have used the farmers' point of view as an example, with being good of a kind or in a role. Lest the example used might mislead, it should be added that being good from a point of view does not necessarily involve being good from the point of view of some particular set of persons, such as the farmers. There are abstract points of view which anybody may adopt. Thus any of us may look at a problem from the agricultural point of view without being farmers. Moreover something may be bad from the agricultural point of view (leading perhaps to low quality crops) but good from the farmers' point of view (leading perhaps to higher profits); in looking at something from the agricultural point of view we are looking at it from an abstract point of view which may or may not impinge specially on the interests of some particular set of persons, not from the other fellow's point of view. There are, if I am correct in what follows, much more obviously abstract points of view than the agricultural.

Since we can ask of anything that can affect any point of view whether it affects a certain point of view and in what way, though the overwhelming majority of things will affect most points of view negligibly or not at all, the expression 'things from a point of view' can name no class. This explains why the question 'Is this a thing from the X point of view?' has no use. It contrasts with the limits on things which can be judged in a certain role and the still narrower limits on things which can be judged as of a certain kind.

It seems to me that many of our uses of 'good' are rather of this type which I have called 'good from a point of view' even when they appear grammatically to conform to the 'good of a kind' specification; certainly the use is not confined to cases which are of the grammatical form 'This is a good thing from the Y point of view'. A few examples will show the sort of cases that I have in mind.

(1) 'This is economically a good thing' is clearly very closely akin to 'This is a good thing from the economic point of view'. We have here a case of judgement from an abstract point of view, and 'thing from a point of view', like 'thing economically', designates no kind.

(2) The same point can be made about 'aesthetically' and 'from the aesthetic point of view'. It is useful to consider the composite example: 'The planting of the hard shoulder of motorways with flowers would be a good thing from the aesthetic point of view (aesthetically), but economically (from the economic point of view) could not be justified'.

(3) Let us take the case of the expressions 'good buy' and 'best buy' as used by the magazine *Which?* (in America *Consumers' Report*). If a certain brand of pen is said to be the best buy it is not being said to be the best pen available, for the best pen might be absurdly over-priced and thus a poor buy. But there is not a class of things called 'buys' within which these magazines make each

month a different choice of the best. It seems that 'This is a good buy' could best be paraphrased in some such way as 'This is good from the prospective purchaser's point of view' and classed as a point of view use of 'good'. A further point brought out by this case should be noted. For reasons not too hard to divine the cost of an article is never treated as a criterion of its merit as of its kind, however important it may be to us in making our choice.

(4) Similar to the case of 'buy' are the cases, or some of the cases, in which we refer to good plans, good choices or good ideas. No doubt an instructor at an Army Staff College might sometimes refer to something as a good plan wishing thereby to grade it highly by the criteria appropriate to the kind 'plan'—criteria such as clarity, logical ordering of its parts and the like. But usually when we say that something is a good plan we mean to commend a possible course of action from the point of view of the prospective agent. The same applies to choices and ideas even more obviously; it would be hard to interpret 'That's a good idea' as a judgement on a member of the kind 'idea' as such. The same point becomes still more obvious if we consider that we often speak of a fine specimen of a motor car, apple or pine tree; but perhaps only a Staff College instructor would ever wish to speak of a fine specimen of a plan, and only an analytic psychologist of a fine specimen of a choice, idea or proposal.

It seems, then, that there clearly is a distinction between evaluations of things as of a kind and from a point of view. Sometimes in an evaluation the criteria which are relevant are determined solely by the character of the object evaluated, by whether it is an apple or golfer or what not that we are judging. These are cases of being good of a kind. But sometimes the relevant standards or criteria of evaluation are determined not by the character of the object evaluated but by the point of view that the judge has adopted, by the interests that he is bearing in mind. These are the cases of being good from a point of view.

Four further general points about this distinction need to be made before we turn to the final and most controversial point of this discussion.

(1) Sometimes one of the criteria for an object being good of a kind is its being good from a certain point of view. Probably one, though only one, of the criteria of merit of dining-room tables is their being good from an aesthetic point of view, whereas being good from an aesthetic point of view is equally probably not taken into account by judges of concrete mixers. Even if one preferred good-looking concrete mixers it would, I suspect, be eccentric to regard a better-looking one as being for that reason a better one. But a better looking dining-room table is clearly, *ceteris paribus*, a better one. This point in no way blurs the distinction that has been made. That one type of evaluation should be relevant to another is not a reason for denying the difference between them.

(2) A better X is more likely to be good from a point of view than is a worse X. But this, while readily intelligible, seems to be a statistical truth and there are exceptions. That the surface of Merton Street, Oxford, is, judged as a surface, bad, is no doubt a good thing from the point of view of its inhabitants, since it helps a bit to keep the street quieter.

(3) Some of our examples have been of the grammatical form 'This is good from the Y point of view' and some of the form 'This is a good thing from the Y point of view'. I do not think that this difference is material to our inquiry. It seems, somewhat paradoxically, that we insert the word 'thing' when what is evaluated is a state of affairs rather than some object or objects. Thus we should say that a table is good from the aesthetic point of view in making a judgement about the table. But if we were commending a table as making all the difference aesthetically to some arrangement of furniture we might well say that it (its presence) was a good thing from the aesthetic point of view. If we say of a road that it is a good thing from the farmers' point of view, it is because our point could be more fully made by saying that the fact that the road is there is a good thing.

(4) As Professor William Frankena pointed out to me, we must

distinguish between saying, from the Y point of view 'This is a good thing' and saying 'This is a good thing from the Y point of view'. In the former case I have adopted the point of view and speak from it; in the latter case I need not, though I may, identify myself with the point of view. Thus I may say that the window having been left unlocked was a good thing from the burglar's point of view, while remaining a respectable citizen; to say that the unlocked window was a good thing, having adopted the burglar's point of view, would be a sign of social depravity. If I merely say that something is a good thing, without telling you from which point of view I am speaking and without it being clear from the context, you will have to seek enlightenment. There is a complication, which I do not now explore further, that the answer may be: 'On balance, having taken into account all relevant points of view'.

So far the notion of being good of a kind has been briefly explained, examples have been given of a use of 'good' which seem impossible to regard as cases of being good of a kind, and a general account of these examples has been given in terms of being good from a point of view. As the last stage of this discussion I wish to suggest that the 'from a point of view' use of 'good' is very important and common in moral contexts. To some extent it must already be obvious that this claim will be made, and if some of the things that I have already said are correct their application, *mutatis mutandis*, to morals is quite obvious. In particular, if the claim that 'from the economic point of view' and 'from the aesthetic point of view' together with 'economically' and 'aesthetically' exemplify this use of 'good' is correct, it can hardly be doubted that the same is true of 'from the moral point of view' and 'morally'. It seems to me that to say that envy is bad is to evaluate it unfavourably from the moral point of view. If a clear account of the criteria relevant to the moral point of view be now demanded I must admit that I cannot give a satisfactory answer to this basic question of moral philosophy. But I can illustrate the sort of thing I have in mind by pointing out that the upholder of one very naive version of utilitarianism might answer that to judge a thing from the moral point of view is to judge it by the sole criterion of its effect on the greatest happiness of the greatest number. We operate happily with a number of concepts of which we cannot give an adequate philosophical account. I cannot give an adequate account of the aesthetic point of view either, or of the economic point of view; writings of welfare economists suggest that nobody else can.

But I now want to make the less obvious, and far more dubious, claim that when we speak of a good man, a good motive or a good deed or action in a moral context we have examples of the 'point of view' use of 'good'. I do feel quite certain that the attempt of the emotivists and many others to assimilate the use of 'good' when applied to men, motives and actions in moral contexts, to that in 'good apple' and 'good motor car' is quite wrong. I feel equally certain that we must not revert to the old fantasy of a special and peculiar meaning of 'good' in moral contexts. The arguments for the view here put forward are not conclusive, but are, I hope, worth consideration. First, then, let me give some reasons for holding that there are important differences between our use of 'good' in, on the one hand, 'good man (woman, angel)', 'good action (deed)', 'good motive' and 'good intention', and, on the other hand, 'good motor car (apple, golfer)'.

(1) Such expressions as 'first rate', 'tip-top', 'high quality', 'top-notch' and 'unrivalled' can be substituted for 'good' in such judgements as 'This is a good golfer (motor car, apple, horse)' without any important change of meaning. 'Unrivalled' is a stronger claim than 'good' but that sort of difference is irrelevant. Possibly 'He is a high quality golfer' rings a bit strange; perhaps because to be a golfer is to figure in a role and not to be of a kind. But even this judgement sounds well when compared with either of the following:

$$\text{He acted from a}\ \begin{cases}\text{top-notch}\\\text{tip-top}\\\text{high quality}\end{cases}\text{motive, } vice \text{ 'good motive'.}$$

$$\text{The road to hell is paved with} \begin{cases} \text{superb specimens of} \\ \text{first class} \\ \text{high grade} \end{cases} \text{intentions.}$$

So we see that substitutions which seem to involve only subtle distinctions when we are speaking of motor cars, golfers and the like become wholly unplausible when we are speaking of motives and intentions in a moral context.

Now let us consider the following assertions:

$$\text{Unlike Lucifer, Gabriel was a} \begin{cases} \text{first class} \\ \text{high grade} \\ \text{top notch} \\ \text{tip-top} \\ \text{very superior} \end{cases} \text{angel.}$$

Each of these makes perfectly idiomatic sense, but only if interpreted non-morally. So interpreted they are false, or could be claimed to be true only on the captious ground that Gabriel was a cherub, Lucifer an archangel. But true or false, their sense is quite different from that of the indisputably true statement that unlike Lucifer Gabriel was a good angel. It is clear, I hope, that the same point can be made with regard to men and women as with regard to angels. We often do wish to talk of first class men; but when we do so it is to make a very different evaluation from that made when we speak of a good man in a moral context.

It is clear that the same point can be made about actions or deeds as has just been made about motives, intentions, men and angels. One might think up some queer context in which it would be natural to speak of a first class action or a high quality deed; but if one did it would not be in the same familiar moral context in which one speaks of a good action or doing a good deed every day.

Here then we have one indication of the difference of our use of 'good' in moral contexts from its use when we speak of something being good of a kind or in a role. We either fall into absurdity, such as we get when we speak of a superb specimen of a motive, or are involved in a complete change of point, such as we get when we speak of a top-notch rather than a good angel, when we substitute for 'good' in moral contexts evaluative terms which can be substituted for 'good' in 'good of a kind' contexts with at the most minor differences in style, emphasis and the like.

(2) We now turn to the second consideration designed to fulfil the same negative end of showing that we must not assimilate the use of 'good' in moral contexts to its use in standard cases of being good of a kind. We have already noticed that we employ different criteria for assessing the merits of examples of different kinds of things. Cats cannot be judged by the criteria appropriate to dogs; knowing how to judge apples is of little aid to one who wishes to assess the merits of a golfer or a power shovel. Again, while there are no doubt different grades of angel, the criteria for assessing which are no doubt to be found in the works of pseudo-Dionysius, men are not to be judged by these criteria in non-moral contexts. If I am a poor specimen of a man it is not because I lack three pairs of wings wherewith to cover my face and feet and to fly.

But in moral contexts the case appears to be quite otherwise. It seems clear that we do judge angels by the same criteria as men in moral contexts. Belial, in *Paradise Lost*, is objectionable morally in the same way as a man would be, and Satan has a certain moral grandeur for the same reason as a man would have moral grandeur. Still more striking from our present point of view, though in many contexts it is no doubt a truism, is the fact that in moral contexts we judge the goodness of men, actions, motives and intentions by the same set of criteria. This truism would surely be a gigantic paradox, when we consider how different in general character all these things are, if we were dealing with straight-forward cases of things being good of a kind.

(3) I now bring a third argument designed to suggest that our use of 'good' in moral contexts does not resemble our use of it in judging things as of a kind. We have noticed evaluative adjectives like 'high quality' and 'top-notch' which we can substitute for 'good' in 'of a kind' contexts but not in moral contexts. We may now observe that there are some adjectives which clearly work in

the same way as 'good' in moral contexts but which are not possible substitutes for 'good' in typical non-moral contexts. The most obvious example is that 'wicked' is treated as an opposite of 'good' in moral contexts; but in non-moral contexts it either cannot be used at all ('wicked apple' sounds decidedly queer) or else is clearly a colloquial transference as when we speak of a wicked shot in golf. But wicked is used quite plainly of men, actions, motives and intentions. The same point can be made about such adjectives as 'worthy' and 'evil', though both are terms which we are chary of using nowadays.

(4) The fourth and final point that I wish to make on this theme is that 'good' is not so closely tied to the noun that follows it (some have said 'substantive-hungry') when we use it of men, actions, motives and intentions in moral contexts as it is when we speak of a good motor car, apple or golfer. As has often been observed, to say that something is a red apple seems to be a compression of the two judgements that the thing is red and that it is an apple; but when we say that something is a good apple the judgement that it is good is not so independent; it is good judged simply as an apple but may be poor judged as a cooker. Now we may certainly speak of a good father or a good husband in such a way that we are considering merit in a role, not making a moral judgement, and 'good' is then closely tied to its noun. No doubt being good from a moral point of view is one criterion for being a good father but it is not the whole story. Someone may be a poor father or husband for reasons of temperament or metabolism which have no bearing on moral character. Further the same man may be a good husband, but a bad father if, say, he spoils his children to a ridiculous extent. But if a woman has a wicked husband then her children must have a wicked father, even if his wickedness is not manifested towards them, and if their father is good in the sense opposed to wicked then her husband must be good in this way also. Thus if one says that Mrs Smith has a wicked husband one is judging someone wicked and identifying him as Mrs Smith's husband, whereas if one speaks of somebody as a bad actor one is not judging him to be bad and incidentally identifying him as an actor.

Thus we should distinguish:

(a) 'X is a good husband' in a use parallel to 'This is a good apple';

(b) 'X is a good husband from the moral point of view', which is to say that X satisfies one important criterion for being a good husband;

(c) 'She has a good husband', as opposed to having a wicked husband, which can be reworded as 'She has a husband and he is morally good'.

I have now produced my four contentions in support of the view that in moral contexts 'good' is not used as when we are judging the merits of things as of a kind or in a role. They are, in brief, that:

(1) Some adjectives which can be used in 'good of a kind' contexts cannot be used of men, actions and motives in moral contexts.

(2) We have different criteria of merit for different kinds of things but the same criteria in moral contexts for all objects of judgement.

(3) Some adjectives, such as 'wicked' and 'worthy', function in the same way as 'good' in moral contexts but have at best a colloquial or figurative use outside moral contexts.

(4) Adjectives such as 'good' and 'wicked' are not substantive-hungry in moral contexts, as are evaluative terms in judgements of merit as of a kind.

It seems to me that none of these points is a proof that there is a great difference between our use of 'good' in moral contexts and its use in 'of a kind' contexts in isolation; but jointly they are a strong indication of something important. Most of these differences can be explained, though not all of them, by taking it that in moral contexts we use 'good' in the way that has earlier been discussed with reference to such examples as 'This is a good thing from the farmers' point of view'. When we say of something that it is a good man, action, intention or motive we are saying of it that it is good from the moral point of view and incidentally identifying it as a man, action, motive or intention.

If we accept that 'good' has, in moral contexts, a 'point of view' use, even when it literally qualifies a noun, we can account readily enough for some of the facts which are anomalous when interpreted on the model of judgements of goodness as of a kind.

First, the explanation of the fact that we have the same criteria of merit for men, actions, intentions and motives simply is that we are judging them all from the same point of view; surely if we are to find any homogeneity in the vast variety of things subject to moral appraisal it derives from the fact that all are being assessed from a single point of view. It would really be quite idle to look for some very general kind of which men, their deeds and their motives were species, and to suggest that we are judging by the criteria appropriate to this kind.

Secondly, the 'point of view' hypothesis accounts readily for the fact that in moral contexts the evaluative adjective is not so closely tied to the noun that follows it as in 'good of a kind' contexts. In the latter type of context the noun is indispensable for showing the scope and criteria of the judgement, whereas in 'good from a point of view' contexts the noun merely helps to identify what is being judged and in no way clarifies the principle of judgement employed. We find the same phenomenon in cases of judgement from other points of view; thus if one says in an art gallery: 'That is a good picture of a man stroking a parrot' one should not be interpreted as saying: 'By the criteria for pictures of men stroking parrots that comes out near the top of the class' but rather: 'That—I mean the picture of a man stroking a parrot—is good from the aesthetic point of view'.

Thirdly, our hypothesis makes it intelligible why we avoid such evaluative terms as 'first rate' and 'high grade' in moral contexts, having as compensation other specialised terms such as 'evil' and 'wicked'. If we use an evaluative adjective with a noun it is immediately tempting to assume that we have an evaluation as of a kind. Therefore, though we may say 'She has a wicked husband' with the confident expectation that we shall be interpreted as making a moral evaluation, we should hesitate to assert the contrary in the form 'She has a good husband', which is naturally taken to be an evaluation within the kind *husband*; we should prefer to say 'Her husband is a good man'. I suggest that we avoid the ambiguity of type of assessment by limiting ourselves to a small selection of nouns like 'man', 'action' and 'motive' in adjective-plus-noun constructions which are to be interpreted in a moral sense; we make matters still clearer by having also a relatively specialised set of evaluative adjectives for use in such contexts.

This point can be further strengthened by noting that we tend also to have specialised evaluative terms for other points of view. 'Useful' and 'valuable' are specialised towards assessment from the economic angle; 'beautiful', 'pretty' and many others are primarily aesthetic. But we should not represent things as being tidier than they are. We speak readily enough of first rate pictures and bargains when judging from the aesthetic or economic point of view; clearly also we use 'good' and 'bad' without any restriction, relying on context to make plain what type of evaluation is involved.

The contention put forward in this chapter has been that we must distinguish a type of evaluation which I have called evaluation from a point of view from evaluation of a kind. That every suggestion made in this chapter has been convincingly established would be a monstrous claim. But at least it seems clear to me that there are distinctions and niceties to be examined in connexion with our use of 'good' which the emotivist theory is far too simple to deal with.

However, if the distinctions we have claimed to find are in general satisfactory we can make some application of them in criticism of the emotivist position. While claiming that standard-using must be distinguished from standard-setting, we have so far allowed to Stevenson that the setting of standards is purely a matter of persuasion. But it seems that in fact we can and do argue for and against the acceptance of certain standards for things being good of a kind by considering whether their acceptance would or would not be a good thing from certain important points of view. Thus we might try to justify the acceptance of certain standards of merit in certain foods by showing that from a nutritional point of view it would be a good thing to accept them; it might be a good thing from the nutritional point of view that having a high fat-content should be a criterion for the merit of cheese (or it might be a bad thing— medical knowledge is relevant here). Perhaps it is a bad thing from the point of view of road safety that high maximum speed should be regarded as a standard for the merit of motor cars. Certainly, in arguing in either of these ways we should be assuming the accept-ability of the safety and nutritional points of view; but then we might be willing to argue for the importance of considering these points of view by adducing considerations derived from the economic point of view. No doubt in any such argument some evaluative position will be used without justification. But it is the common fate of arguments in all fields to assume the validity of some premisses or principles of argument. No doubt a finite evaluative argument must make some unargued evaluative assump-tions, just as finite factual arguments must make some unargued factual assumptions. Neither of these facts should be a matter for wonder, nor is the unargued necessarily unjustifiable.

10

A TEST FOR EVALUATIVE TERMS

We have, in the last two chapters, seen reason to doubt the emotivist
claim that a single account of all evaluative terms can be given, on
the ground that they vary only in nuance of emotion expressed and
evoked or in ways of more interest to the student of English idiom
than to the philosopher. But which terms are evaluative? Clearly
the term 'good' is the paradigm which has an undisputed claim for
inclusion in the class; if 'good' is not an evaluative term then no
term is. But how widely does the class extend? We shall first
examine the answers given by the emotivists to this question and
then, having found them wanting, attempt to give a more satisfactory one of our own.

   If we take it that an evaluative term is one that has emotive meaning and accept the definition of emotive meaning given on page 59
of *Ethics and Language*: 'Emotive meaning is a meaning in which
the response (from the hearer's point of view) or the stimulus
(from the speaker's point of view) is a range of emotions', then an
enormous and heterogeneous set of terms will be evaluative for
some people. If a judgement is evaluative if it contains evaluative
terms then there will be a correspondingly wide set of evaluative
judgements. It would be hard to think of any term, other than
articles, pronouns, prepositions and the like, that does not sometimes stimulate an emotion in somebody or other. It is unclear
whether Stevenson would wish to claim that all such terms and
judgements are evaluative. On page 211 of *Ethics and Language*

he says: 'Further explanation [of persuasive definition] can best proceed by example, and at first examples will be taken from terms that are, so to speak, only semi-ethical—terms which are not usually given the unqualified ethical status of "good", "right", "duty" and "ought", but which introduce many of the same considerations'; he then gives examples in which the persuasively defined 'semi-ethical' terms are 'culture' (p. 211), 'poet' (p. 213), 'charity' (p. 213), 'courage', 'sportsmanship', 'genius' and 'beauty' (all on p. 214). But what is here meant by 'ethical' and 'semi-ethical'? If 'ethical' means something like 'exclusively (or pre-eminently) used in ethical contexts', it is hard to see why 'good' and 'right' should be called ethical but not 'courage' and 'charity', which seem to belong far more exclusively and preeminently to ethical contexts. Moreover in any natural sense of 'ethical' it is hard to see why 'culture', 'genius' and 'beauty' are semi-ethical terms; none seems to be used frequently in ethical contexts and 'beauty' might well be accorded, in Stevenson's terminology, 'unqualified aesthetic status'. The only tolerable explanation is to take it that here, and indeed regularly, Stevenson means by 'ethical' simply 'evaluative'; in this usage 'That is a beautiful picture' will be an ethical judgement. It will now be plausible to suppose that the terms 'good', 'right', 'duty' and 'ought' are given unqualified ethical (i.e. evaluative) status because they can be used in evalua-tions whatever the subject matter whereas the 'semi-ethical' terms in some way or other are restricted to certain fields of evaluation. It would require just a little ingenuity to bring the terms 'charity' and 'sportsmanship' into a discussion of power shovels, whereas one can easily refer to a good power shovel or the duties of a power shovel operator.

But this way of distinguishing between the wholly and the semi-evaluative is unsatisfactory, whether it is or is not what Stevenson intended. On this interpretation 'wicked' will be semi-ethical or semi-evaluative, since it is as confined to moral contexts as 'beautiful' is to aesthetic contexts; so 'he is a good man' will be wholly evaluative but its contradictory 'he is a wicked man' will be only semi-evaluative. Or, again, into which category does 'valid' fall?

It can be used of arguments, objections, marriages, wills, contracts, procedures and a host of other disparate things; but its range is not so wide as that of 'good'. Are we then to count it as an evaluative or semi-evaluative term? Is it an evaluative term at all? Some say it is and some say it is not, but Stevenson on our conjectural interpretation gives us no help at all towards settling the issue.

Let us now turn to Mr Richard Robinson's contribution to the symposium on the emotive theory of ethics, to be found in the Supplementary Volume of the Aristotelian Society of 1948, for enlightenment. He says there that the name 'the emotive theory of ethics' 'must mean some theory which implies that a word may also have independent emotive meaning. Independent emotive meaning is the power of a word to arouse emotion independently of what it describes and names.' He adds that the name 'emotive theory of ethics' also implies the view that ethical words have independent emotive meaning. Now it is clear that Robinson is using 'ethical' in the surprisingly generous sense in which Stevenson also used it, for he says that he wants to include 'beautiful' and 'charming' as ethical terms or else is willing to speak not of the emotive theory of ethics but the emotive theory of axiology. Now on Robinson's view 'nigger' has independent emotive meaning (independent of the object also named without emotive meaning by 'negro'); but he would not wish to count 'nigger' as an ethical or axiological term so he adds the requirement that ethical or axiological terms purport to name non-natural qualities, but in fact name no quality. We have here an instance of the 'error theory', according to which ordinary users of certain evaluative terms think that in using them they are ascribing qualities to objects, and are mistaken in so thinking. A statement of this theory can also be found in Mackie's 'The Refutation of Morals' in the *Australasian Journal of Psychology and Philosophy* for 1946; it was held by Carritt about 'beauty', but not about 'goodness'; it is critically discussed in Edwards, *The Logic of Moral Discourse*, chapter III. But we cannot incorporate the error theory into a definition of evaluative terms, not because the theory is false, but because we cannot accept a definition of evaluative terms such that if the theory is false there will be no evaluative terms. If evaluative terms were ones which people used with erroneous beliefs, but people never used terms with such erroneous beliefs, then there would be no evaluative terms. Moreover, it is not clear of what terms the theory is supposed to be true; once again, does 'valid' purport to describe or designate some bogus non-natural quality, and how do we find out whether it does? So, on Robinson's own view independent emotive meaning is not enough to mark off axiological terms and the extra requirements are not acceptable as a criterion of the axiological. Indeed, in fairness we must note that the requirements are stated by Robinson as part of a definition of the emotive theory of ethics and not as a criterion of an axiological term. He himself says: 'We cannot ... find an easy method of determining whether any given word is ethical.'

There is, so far as I have been able to discover, no clear account anywhere of the range of terms that their theory was intended to cover. We must, therefore, make an independent investigation to attempt to remedy the defect. But since the term 'evaluative' as we are using it and as it is commonly used in philosophy is a term of art without a settled usage, there is no question of finding a correct account to the exclusion of all others. If we can find some reasonably clear criterion which will include in the evaluative class such terms the application of which to a thing in a typical context would naturally be called grading, commending, assessing merit (or something similar) and exclude others we may be content.

But some issues with which we are faced cannot be settled in any very natural way. For example, (a) do we want to include both 'good' and 'right' as evaluative terms, or do we want to mark the considerable difference between them already noted by calling the one, say, evaluative and the other normative? (b) do we want to include terms like 'brave', 'charitable' and 'just' as evaluative? (c) do we want to include such terms as 'poet', 'culture', 'scholar' and 'leader' as evaluative? (d) do we want to include such terms as 'nigger', 'old maid', 'nark', 'yid' and 'wop' as evaluative? (e) should we include such verbal forms as 'I approve of', 'I commend' and 'I recommend'? Such questions as these cannot be answered as a matter of right and wrong, though, as in botanical classification, one decision may be wiser than another. I should regard a criterion of 'evaluative' as absurd only if it excluded the term 'good' and its cognates, which should be regarded as the paradigmatic case.

Let us consider the first four of the five questions just raised, temporarily postponing the fifth. The first question for decision is whether we are to have a very general account of evaluation, to include all that could count as coming out in favour of a thing or against it, or whether to limit it to scalar assessment of merit, excluding the right-or-wrong, correct-or-incorrect, hit-or-miss type of adjudication. Provided that there is here both a generic similarity and specific difference, it is a matter of practical judgement, not theoretical discernment which we now attend to. But, whereas both rightness and goodness are questions that may arise in almost any field of assessment, the terms in our second group, such as 'brave' and 'charitable', are not so context-free. Two stories of bravery or charity must have some closer similarity than two stories of rightness or goodness need have. It is tempting to say that 'brave' means something like 'good in frightening contexts' and 'charitable' something like 'good in the matter of giving'. We might say that the terms in the second class indicate excellence or rightness, or the reverse, in a restricted field. Terms in the third class, such as 'poet', 'culture', 'scholar' and 'leader', present a particularly difficult problem. A great number of terms, including the names of crafts and skills, can only be applied where a certain minimum of competence has been achieved. One could not be called a tightrope walker merely in virtue of habitually putting one's feet on a tightrope and at once falling off, and a cyclist must have some capacity for staying on his machine. Would one be a versifier, let alone a poet, if one's compositions could not be recognised as being even verse? Are we then to regard 'tightrope walker' and 'cyclist' as evaluative terms, and 'versifier' to have as great a claim to be counted in as 'poet'? There is no easy solution to this difficulty. On the one hand, while 'Ramm was not a pianist but an oboe player' would naturally be taken as a mere piece of musical history, we may well say of someone who frequently sits at the piano 'He

E

is no pianist' with a clear evaluative intent. On the other hand one could in many contexts assert that Whittier was a poet and not to be confused with the painter Whistler without having committed oneself to any evaluation of the verses of Whittier. Thus terms like 'poet' and 'leader', even when used in a clearly evaluative way, are evaluative because of the context of their utterance, whereas 'brave' and 'charitable' were restricted in their application to certain types of context, but their evaluative force did not depend on the context of their utterance.

I should certainly wish to exclude the terms in our fourth class, such as 'nigger' and 'old maid', from the class of evaluative terms, even though 'nigger' and 'old maid' are two of the most common examples of words with emotive meaning in the literature. Such terms are certainly derogatory, slighting, impolite or pejorative; similarly we have terms which are euphemistic or flattering. But if a negro is referred to as a nigger, an elderly spinster as an old maid or a policeman as a flattie one can only deplore the choice of terminology, one cannot express disagreement with the content of the assertion as one can disagree with an evaluation. If I refer to a wicked negro as a good nigger you can reply that I falsely call him good; but my use of the term 'nigger' is unfortunate, mean or ill-bred, not false. You may say that I should not call him a nigger, but not that he is not a nigger. Though we have seen ground to exclude such terms as 'poet' from the evaluative class, in their case we can at least refuse to accept the term 'poet' or 'scholar' as applicable, rather than merely objecting to choice of vocabulary. Indeed, many of the terms which are now deplored, such as old maid, are deplored merely because they are not euphemisms; it is much like the situation we are in at the national level: states which once were called undeveloped later had to be called, in politeness, underdeveloped, and then again developing. So, even though we may sometimes infer that the choice of a coarse or vulgar name arises from some animosity towards or contempt for its bearer, we must not confuse flattery, politeness, impoliteness, arrogance and the like with evaluation.

We have seen, then, that there is no one correct criterion of an evaluative term and that not all philosophers would agree what terms a criterion should exclude and which it should include. But if it be agreed at least that the terms 'good' and 'bad' and their comparatives 'better', 'best', 'worse' and 'worst' are the paradigmatic cases, so that if it is proper to call any terms evaluative it is proper to call these evaluative, we might seek for a criterion expressed in terms of them. Let us say that a term V is favourably evaluative if, and only if, it would be an abuse of language to deny that in so far as a thing is V it is better than a non-V thing, and a term is unfavourably evaluative if, and only if, it would be an abuse of language to deny that in so far as a thing is U it is worse than a non-U thing. We must take the notion of an abuse of language to exclude the wildest degree of oddness and eccentricity of a non-verbal kind. Thus it can be denied without abuse of language that sixpence is better than nothing since it would be prudential folly, rather than linguistic abuse, to prefer to be penniless than to have sixpence. Thus 'sixpence' and 'nothing' are not evaluative terms according to our criterion, which is intuitively acceptable.

Let us, then, test our criterion on some of the terms which have been from time to time suggested to be evaluative in the literature.

(1) In so far as a thing is good it is better than what is not good.

(2) In so far as a thing is right it is better than what is not right.

(3) In so far as a thing is brave it is better than what is not brave.

(4) In so far as a thing is charitable it is better than what is not charitable.

(5) In so far as a thing is just it is better than what is not just.

I think that it would be an abuse of language to deny any of these examples, if they are understood in a straightforward way. No doubt the case will be different if we suppose there to be 'sneer quotes' round the valuative term, making it equivalent to 'what is conventionally regarded as good (right, just, etc.)', but this need no more disturb us than the fact that in sneering sarcasm many non-evaluative terms imply the opposite of their dictionary meanings. We could not simply say, however, that what is brave, right, just or charitable is better than what is not. For what is brave, for example, might on occasion have so many other bad features that it could be said without abuse of language to be worse than a non-brave alternative; however, in so far as an action was brave it would be better than one which was not, whatever our judgement would be, all things considered.

It is surely clear that the same holds with regard to the un-favourable opposites of the examples given. Thus it would be an abuse of language to deny that in so far as something is wrong it is worse than what is not wrong. It is clear, also, that there is as strong a case for regarding such context-free adjectives as 'useful', 'admirable', 'high-quality' and their opposites as evaluative as there is for 'good' and 'right'. Moreover, if we allow 'brave' and 'just' we can hardly exclude other terms ascriptive of virtues and vices.

Let us now look at some examples from our fourth class.

(6) In so far as somebody is a nigger he is worse than somebody who is not.

(7) In so far as somebody is an old maid she is worse than somebody who is not.

(8) In so far as somebody is a nark he is worse than somebody who is not.

It seems that all of these are non-evaluative by our present test, for there would be no linguistic absurdity in denying the lot, though there might be some statistical likelihood that anyone who was prepared to utter them seriously would accept them. But if somebody were to say 'Any nigger is better than any white trash any day' we could deplore his coarse language and racial bigotry without claiming to find any conceptual paradoxes in his speech.

This result is in accordance with the preference for excluding such terms to which I have already admitted. No doubt the emotivist is right in claiming that we can express our emotions by using such terms; but we need to distinguish evaluation from vulgar abuse and flattery.

If we turn our attention to the third class of terms we get examples such as the following:

(9) In so far as somebody is a poet he is better than somebody who is not.

(10) In so far as somebody is a scholar he is better than some-body who is not.

(11) In so far as somebody is a leader he is better than somebody who is not.

On a straightforward interpretation all these examples exhibit wild enthusiasm, and each can be contradicted without any absurdity. To assent to example 9, for instance, is to commit oneself to the view that it is a defect in a person not to be a poet. To be capable of writing poetry is no doubt an accomplishment that nobody should spurn, like every other accomplishment; but it is absurd to regard it as a defect in Beethoven that he did not in fact write poetry. Even if we interpret the example to mean 'Among those who write verses, in so far as one is a poet he is better than one who is not', there is no obvious linguistic absurdity in denying it. If somebody prefers satirical verse that makes no pretence to poetical merit to poetry in the narrow sense we may disagree with him, but can hardly convict him of linguistic absurdity if he claims that some versifiers who are not poets are better than some who are. No doubt we should grade more highly those who succeed in being poets among those who try to be poets; but this is no more significant than the fact that we should grade higher those who succeed in drawing corks than those who try but fail. As we have already noted, it would be idle to deny that very often when people speak of a real leader, a true poet or a genuine scholar their remarks are to be construed as being in their context evaluative.

But this should no more make us regard 'poet', 'leader' and 'scholar' as evaluative terms than the fact that 'Now that *is* a (real) cup of tea' is often said appreciatively should make us regard 'cup of tea' as evaluative.

If we now turn to our fifth class of terms, which comprises such terms as 'approve of', 'commend' and 'recommend', we shall find ourselves faced with difficulties which we have so far studiously avoided and will require a whole new discussion of basic issues. Whatever criticisms we have so far made of the emotivist theory, and they have been many, we have not so far found reason to challenge the claim that evaluative terms can be valuably clarified in terms of approval, commendation, recommendation and the like. We have, indeed, as the emotivists themselves insisted, denied that 'This is good' can be construed as meaning the same as 'I approve of this'. But we have noticed that anyone who expresses approval of a thing or commends it cannot in consistency deny that it is good and that anyone who says that something is good can be construed as committing himself thereby to a favourable attitude of approval or commendation or something similar. Indeed, if one wishes to express approval or commendation of a thing, to say that it is good seems one of the most obvious ways of doing so. Thus the link between goodness and these favourable attitudes seems to be very close.

But it is abundantly clear that according to our criterion 'approve', 'commend', 'recommend' and the like are not evaluative terms. The assertion

(12) In so far as you approve of (commend, recommend) a thing it is better than what you do not approve of (commend, recommend)

can not merely be denied without absurdity; it sounds a quite ridiculous thing to say. If we respect your judgement we may regard your approval as a reason for expecting its object to be good, but your approval is not in itself a merit of the thing, as, say, the bravery of an action is a merit whatever other defects it may have. An example in the third person ('he approves') would clearly lead to results no different.

Now we have already noted that in the case of verbs like 'approve of' and 'commend' what we have to say about their use in the first person is often very different from what must be said of them in other persons. But on the present topic the case is not essentially different if we take examples in the first person singular.

(13) In so far as I approve of (commend, recommend) a thing it is better than what I do not approve of (commend, recommend)

sounds merely like a piece of demented arrogance. Anyone with any humility will readily admit that he has often approved of and commended things which were bad and made no better by the fact that he had approved of or commended them. We need not withdraw our acknowledgment that one who approves of or commends a thing is committed in consistency to claiming that it is good until he withdraws his approval or commendation. But that is another matter which does not affect the present issue.

So, it appears, 'approve', 'commend' and 'recommend' are not evaluative terms according to our criterion. One possible line that may be taken by anybody who finds this result disconcerting is to claim that it merely shows the inadequacy of our criterion. I have already made it clear that I lay no great weight on the criterion and can easily be induced to alter the details of its formulation, which may well be faulty. Thus it may be claimed that A— is a favourably evaluative term in its use as applied to examination papers. But if we consider

(14) In so far as a paper is A— it is better than a paper which is not A— there is the obvious objection that such a paper is not better than one which is A, and that what is A is not A—. Faced with this I should not deny that A— was evaluative but should attempt to revise the criterion in detail. Perhaps

(15) In so far as a paper is A— it is better than a paper which is not at least A—

will suffice. But this is a point of detail. The essence of the criterion
is that if a thing can be favourably evaluated in any way, has any
sort of merit, that must count as a reason, though not a conclusive
reason, for counting it as good. 'Approve', 'commend' and 'recommend' do not fail here because of remediable technical difficulties
such as we found in the case of A—, but quite decisively.

Another theoretically possible expedient would be to claim that
'good' is not a completely general but a specialised evaluative term.
Clearly

(16) In so far as an action is brave it is more just than an action
which is not brave

can be denied without absurdity, and yet we do not regard this as
a reason for denying that both 'just' and 'brave' are evaluative
terms. The fact is simply that the specialised merit of bravery does
not necessarily carry with it the specialised merit of justice. But
this theoretical possibility has nothing to recommend it, for the
generality of 'good' is something which lexicographers and philosophers have often noted and which no one has given any reason to
doubt.

However, whatever plausibility our criterion may have in
principle, if not in detail, its failure to admit 'approve', 'commend'
and 'recommend' as evaluative terms is not something which we
can regard as disposing of the matter. We have seen reason to
connect these notions intimately with that of evaluation, and we
cannot accept the verdict of our criterion with pious docility and
pass on to new topics. If this verdict is just we must see why it is
just, and this exploration requires us to reopen the whole question
how far the concepts of approval and commendation can be regarded
as shedding light on the concept of goodness. In recent years very
strong arguments have been brought forward in favour of the view
that to regard the concept of goodness as being in any way ex-
plicable in terms of that of approval is a fundamental error. So far
I have studiously avoided any consideration of these arguments,
an avoidance which has very likely irritated and alienated such

readers as are already aware of them. We can no longer afford to leave these arguments on one side, but must examine them both for their own sake and in order to see if they will help us out of the difficulties in which we now find ourselves.

MEANING AND ILLOCUTIONARY FORCE

The emotive theorists claimed that they were giving an account of the meaning of the term 'good'. In examining their views we have not so far considered any challenge to this general view of the nature of their activities. We have accepted it as a correct account of what they were doing and considered only how far they could be regarded as successful in their task. In the course of this examination we have emended their account in several particulars, ending up with some such account as that to say that something is good is to commend, approve of, recommend, grade highly (and so on according to context) that thing in the light of certain recognised criteria either for the kind to which it belongs or from the point of view which we have adopted; we are not now concerned with accuracy of detail. Throughout, the claim has been that in giving these accounts we are explaining the meaning of 'good' in a way which accounts for what Stevenson called its dynamic or magnetic character and which offers a satisfactory alternative to the view that 'good' must stand for some quality in things, natural or non-natural.

But according to some philosophers the belief that we have here even an inaccurate account of the meaning of 'good' is a complete confusion. Some of these philosophers would allow that we have before us an at least roughly true account of something, but claim that we have not got an account of the meaning of 'good' at all. The two most influential discussions on this matter are those of

Ziff in his book *Semantic Analysis* (Cornell University Press, 1960) and Searle in his article 'Meaning and Speech Acts' (in *Knowledge and Experience*, Ed. Rollins, University of Pittsburgh Press, 1962). I shall endeavour to put the main points in my own words, though with much indebtedness both in general and on detailed points to both these authors.

It will be recalled that, in discussing the accounts given by the emotivists of emotive meaning, we had occasion to make use of Austin's distinction between perlocutionary and illocutionary force. For example, the utterance 'Down with the aristocrats' may, in a certain context, have the illocutionary force of *incitement* to revolution; this illocutionary force of incitement we contrasted with perlocutionary force; for example, the utterance 'Down with the aristocrats' might have the perlocutionary force of *provoking* or *exciting* a revolution. Our claim was that whereas illocutionary force was determined by convention, the perlocutionary effects of an utterance were in no way determined by convention; the conclusion drawn was that, since meaning is conventional, the illocutionary force rather than perlocutionary effects should be used in defining emotive meaning.

But Austin also contrasted both illocutionary and perlocutionary force with locutionary force or meaning. If 'Down with the aristocrats' is incitement to revolution at least partly in virtue of its meaning, it is not an account of the meaning of 'Down with the aristocrats' to say that it is an incitement to revolution. Again 'This is yours' may in one context have the illocutionary force of making a gift, in another of stating a fact, in another of giving a verdict, but it would be bizarre to claim that we have just distinguished three possible meanings of the expression 'This is yours'. I may fully understand the meaning of 'Don't give it to him' but fail to discover whether when uttered on some occasion I should construe it as an order, as advice, or as an entreaty. Conversely, I might recognise from the tone of voice, the gestures and the rest of the context that something said to me in a foreign language had the illocutionary force of an order but be quite ignorant of the meaning of the utterance. Thus it seems that we must distinguish the meaning of an utterance from its illocutionary force on a particular occasion; to give the illocutionary force of an utterance is not to give its meaning, and still more obviously not to give the meaning of any particular word in the utterance. To tell me that 'Give me that book' was, on a certain occasion of its utterance, an order, would not be to give an explanation of the meaning of the word 'book'.

Now let us apply these points to the question of the meaning of the word 'good'. It might be conceded to be true and well worth noting that 'This is a good X' has often the illocutionary force of commendation or recommendation, of approval or praise; but once again we have to say that to give the illocutionary force of an utterance is not to give its meaning and that still more obviously to give the illocutionary force of an utterance 'This is a good X' is not to give the meaning of the word 'good' which occurs in that utterance. Single words, except in the special case of such one-word utterances as 'Go!' which might have the illocutionary force of ordering or advising, do not have an illocutionary force.

Moreover, the argument continues, while utterances of the form 'This is a good X' commonly are used with the illocutionary force of some kind of favourable evaluation, and while the expression 'This is a good X' has a reasonably constant meaning, the expression itself cannot be said to have the illocutionary force of evaluation and is not always used with that illocutionary force. When the expression occurs in a subordinate clause it is not used with any illocutionary force. If somebody says 'If the Victoria is a good plum we should plant it ourselves' the whole utterance has no doubt an illocutionary force, but we cannot ask for the illocutionary force of 'The Victoria is a good plum' as it occurs here. Further, we clearly cannot construe the utterance to mean the same as 'If we favourably evaluate the Victoria plum we should plant it'; we should plant it because of its own nature, not because we have made a (possibly erroneous) judgement about it. But we cannot say that 'The Victoria is a good plum' has a different meaning in such a subordinate clause from that which it has when used on its own to make a favourable evaluation. For the argument 'If the

Victoria is a good plum we should plant it; but it is a good plum; therefore we should plant it' is clearly a valid argument. But the argument would not be valid unless the expression 'The Victoria is a good plum' was used with the same meaning in both premisses of the argument. The fact that it might be used with the illocutionary force of favourable evaluation in the second premiss but has no illocutionary force of its own in the first must therefore be irrelevant to its meaning and, therefore, to the meaning of the word 'good' which occurs in it.

But it is not merely the case that 'This is a good X' cannot have an illocutionary force of favourable evaluation in a subordinate clause; there is no necessity that the expression 'This is a good X' should be used with an evaluative illocutionary force even when it forms a complete utterance, even if it is often so used. Let us suppose that I ask you to meet a girl for me at the railway station and that you ask for a description of her so that you may recognise her. 'Well', I say, 'she is tall, dark, always wears a hat, has a good figure, etcetera.' Surely my assertion here that she has a good figure is just part of a description; in saying this I am describing her so that you will recognise her. I might have said 'she has a good figure' as praise if you were reluctant to do me the service but were known to be susceptible to feminine charms; but as it is I have no need to interrupt my utilitarian description in order to insert an irrelevant encomium.

So not merely does the expression 'This is a good X' not have any illocutionary force of its own, but when used to make a complete utterance with some illocutionary force need not have a favourably evaluative illocutionary force. Commending and the like are just some among the illocutionary forces that 'This is a good X' may have, not an essential feature of the meaning of 'good'.

Further, just as 'This is a good X' may or may not have a favourably evaluative illocutionary force, according to context, the same is true of expressions in which what we have so far taken to be purely descriptive terms are substituted for 'good'. 'This is a very light whisky' (whatever it may mean) often appears in advertisements so that it is unmistakably intended to be a recommendation or praise. One may say the washing is snow-white, that the silver is bright or that the fruit is juicy in such tones and in such a context that the remark has to be construed as praise or commendation. So, it would appear, the occurrence of 'good' or some other of what we have called so far evaluative terms is neither a necessary nor a sufficient condition of the utterance having the force of evaluation.

There is a distinction, the clarification of which we owe to the linguistician Saussure, between speech (*la parole*) and language (*la langue*). Roughly, a language is a tool shared by a group of people who are able to communicate with each other; each of the group has to learn to use it and may use it correctly or incorrectly; speech is the activity in which people engage when using that tool which is their language. Speech and language are of very disparate character; thus of the sentence of the English language 'The queen is dead' we can say such things as that it is grammatically well formed, that it means such and such, that it contains one noun and that it contains four words. But one cannot ask whom this sentence, considered merely as a sentence of the English language, is about, and consequently one cannot ask whether it is true or false. If I use this sentence in my activity of speaking then of my statement, which is a speech act, one can say that it is true if I am referring to Queen Anne but false if I am speaking of Queen Elizabeth II. Questions of meaning and of syntax are questions about sentences, which are linguistic complexes; questions of reference and truth are questions about speech.

Now it seems that the question of the meaning of the word 'good', or the meaning of any other word, is a question about a unit in the vocabulary of the English language. But questions about illocutionary force seem to be questions about speech. We can ask the meaning of a sentence containing the word 'good', but it is only of a use of that sentence in speech, of a speech act, that we may ask whether it was an evaluation. There is no need for surprise if we have found the insistence on the expression and invitation of approval and commendation in the writings of the philosophers whom we have been studying of value. In the study of ethical discourse, of the speech acts which appear in discussion of moral issues, it is no doubt of importance to insist that many ethical utterances have to be construed as expressions of approval and commendation; probably the discussion of these aspects of moral discourse have traditionally been sadly neglected. The insights, we may acknowledge have been valuable; but their value has been diminished by treating them as insights into the meaning of ethical terms, which they are not, instead of insights into the use we make of language in speech. 'In saying that it was good he was commending it' may often be a true and important thing to say; but it is not an account of the meaning of the word 'good'.

The foregoing is, I hope and believe, a fair statement of the argument against the attempt to explain the meaning of 'good' and other terms by reference to approval and commendation. It is not to be supposed that either Ziff or Searle would agree to every detail of its presentation, but their own versions are readily available. One quotation from Ziff will at least establish a close resemblance of some of his argument to my version:

It may be supposed that there is a correlation between the uttering of the word 'good' and a performance of the act of commending. Just so, it may be supposed that there is a correlation between the uttering of the word 'red' and a performance of the act of describing. Thus it has been said that 'good' is a 'term of commendation', that 'red' is a 'descriptive term' and I suppose that this is a way of saying that there is a significant correlation between the uttering of 'good' and the act of commending, between the uttering of 'red' and the act of describing. But such correlations are not in fact to be found.

If one asks (101)

(101) Is that a good red pigment?
one is uttering the words 'red' and 'good' yet one is neither commending nor describing: on the contrary, one is performing the act of asking a question.

It seems to me that the facts about speech and language drawn on in the argument we have just outlined are in general correct. It seems to me also that the accusation that the emotivists and many other philosophers (I am ready to be included among them) have often confused the task of stating the facts about the speech acts typical of ethical discourse with the task of giving an account of the meaning of such terms as 'good' and 'right' is also just. So much I propose to concede without further discussion. But there are certain conclusions that have frequently been drawn from this line of argument which do not seem to follow so clearly. One conclusion is that it is incorrect to attempt to recognise any class of evaluative terms or terms of commendation as Ziff calls them; the other is that not merely must the illocutionary force of utterances be distinguished from the meaning of words but that any reference to the illocutionary force of utterances is irrelevant to an account of the meaning of a word. These two theses need further discussion. Upon this discussion will depend our view about how serious are the implications of this new argument for the kind of theory we have been discussing. Have we revealed defects in its presentation or is it wholly irrelevant to the issues with which it purports to deal?

First of all, we should acknowledge that parts of the argument have been carried to extravagant lengths by some of its more zealous advocates. We have noted that Ziff holds that 'good' cannot be called a term of commendation because, though it occurs in the utterance 'Is this a good red pigment?', we have here not an act of commending but of questioning. But on page 33 of *Semantic Analysis* Ziff says, in my opinion very reasonably, that 'in everyday discourse "ungrammatical" is a term of criticism'. Yet, borrowing Ziff's own weapons, we could retort to him that since the utterance 'Is "men is fat" ungrammatical?' should be construed as an act of questioning and not of criticism it is incorrect to call 'ungrammatical' a term of criticism. By this line of attack we could easily prove that there are no terms of commendation, no terms of criticism, no terms of abuse, no terms of endearment and just about no terms of anything whatsoever. But it is clear that when we call 'ungrammatical' a term of criticism and when we call 'good' a term of commendation, as the Oxford English Dictionary does, we are not making the absurd claim that the term 'ungrammatical' occurs only in critical remarks and 'good' only in acts of commendation, nor the uninteresting and probably false statistical claim that these terms occur in contexts of criticism or commendation more frequently than in other types of context. Just what feature is being brought to our attention by those who speak of a term of commendation, criticism, abuse or endearment is still far from clear; but it is something which is not just an invention of the philosophers, for these expressions are not technical terms of philosophy. If our philosophical arguments lead us to the conclusion that these expressions are out of order, so much the worse for the arguments.

It is clear that 'The door is open' may be used to state a fact, as an expression of incredulity, as a hint to somebody to shut it, and in many other ways. Yet getting clear on these matters seems utterly irrelevant to determining the meaning of the English sentence 'The door is open'. But it is not so clear that all illocutionary forces are always irrelevant in all ways to the meaning of terms. Such an utterance as 'He promised me ten shillings for the cats' home' might be an exclamation of surprise, a hint to you to do the same, or a piece of biographical narration, and to be aware of this does not advance us far towards an understanding of the word 'promise'. Further, if I say that 'I promise to do so and so' has the illocutionary force of binding oneself to perform an action I am not explaining the meaning of the word 'promise' but the force of an utterance. But is an awareness of this (approximate) truth about the force of a certain type of utterance irrelevant to an understanding of the meaning of the word 'promise'? Clearly not; if a Martian were to approach us and say 'While I have a good working knowledge of English I still do not understand the meaning of "promise"' this is just the sort of thing that we should have to teach him. To put it crudely, the word 'promise' exists in order that by its insertion in certain linguistic and non-linguistic contexts we can make it clear that we are performing a speech act with a certain force, and if one does not understand this one does not understand the word. Certainly the expression 'I promise' can come into the question 'Shall I promise . . ?' or be part of a subordinate clause 'If I promise. . . .', and in such a case the utterance

of 'I promise' does not have the illocutionary force of binding oneself, but it is merely silly to think that this shows that the illocutionary force of binding oneself has no special relevance to the
meaning of 'promise'.

So the illocutionary force of some utterances sometimes has no
relevance to the meaning of the words they contain, and the
understanding of some illocutionary forces of some utterances in
some contexts is highly relevant to the understanding of some terms
therein contained. So the fact that the utterance 'Is this good?'
does not have the force of commendation or any other type of
evaluation does not show that we cannot explain the meaning of
'good' in terms of such forces, nor does the fact that 'This is good'
sometimes has the force of commendation show that we can or
must. There is no universal answer to the question whether a
knowledge of illocutionary forces is necessary to the understanding
of a word. We must look at the individual cases. Let us then
consider whether, while admitting the truths brought forward
earlier in this chapter, we still ought to claim that the explanation
of the meaning of the term 'good' involves reference to such
illocutionary forces as commendation.

I suggest that if we consider the range of illocutionary forces
that an utterance may have we may distinguish therein a sub-range
of what I propose to call central and a sub-range of what I propose
to call peripheral forces. I call an illocutionary force central if anyone
who assented to the utterance with any illocutionary force could
not consistently dissent from it when used with that illocutionary
force. An illocutionary force is peripheral if not central, that is, if
assent to the utterance with some illocutionary force is compatible
with dissent from it with this illocutionary force. This distinction
requires both qualification and explanation. It is to be qualified to
exclude certain types of sarcastic, ironic and sneering utterances
where the words used are not to be taken at their face value. There
is nothing unusual about this; if, using the familiar concept of
logical compatibility, one says that 'You've done a lot of work this
morning' is incompatible with 'You've done no work this morning'
one is tacitly excluding the case in which 'You've done a lot of

work this morning' is used sarcastically to mean much the same as 'You've done no work this morning'. Similarly, when I claim that factual narration is a central illocutionary force of the utterance 'you are observing the speed-limit' in that anyone who assented to the utterance with the force of praise or as an exclamation of surprise or any other 'normal' force could not dissent from the utterance as factual narration, it is obviously not the case that assent to the utterance as a sarcasm to one who is wildly exceeding the limit requires assent to the utterance as factual narration.

Some further explanation of the notions of 'assent' and 'dissent' is also necessary. First, I am using them widely so that they cover not only agreement with the utterances of others, which is their most natural meaning, but also independent assertion. Second, when I speak of being unable to dissent from an utterance with a certain force, this has to be distinguished from dissent from the uttering of it with that force. Thus I should say that assent to the utterance of 'There is a bull in that field' as a warning is inconsistent with dissent from it as a factual narration. This contrasts with the fact that assent to 'There is a lamb in that field' with the force of factual narrative is consistent with dissent from the same utterance put forward as a warning. But I do not wish to deny that the uttering of 'There is a bull in that field' as a piece of casual narrative when an ignorant and defenceless person is about to enter it might rightly meet with indignant protests on the score of callous indifference to his safety. We have here a special case of the familiar distinction between agreement with what is said and agreement with the saying of it.

I should claim that any utterance which may bear the force of factual narration must have that force as a central one. If one assents to 'The door is open' as an exclamation of surprised incredulity one cannot dissent from it as a piece of factual narrative, whereas someone who assented to 'The door is open' as factual narrative might regard that same utterance as an exclamation of incredulity as wholly unwarranted and repudiate it. Further I should be disinclined to admit that anyone who could not see this was clear about the meaning of 'The door is open'.

I think that this distinction of central and peripheral forces, if sound, is worth a very general investigation. It is possible that we might find some general logic of implications of illocutionary forces to put alongside our existing logic. But it is not now the time to indulge in this general survey. The distinction must be applied to our present problem. I suggest that favourable evaluative force will be a central illocutionary force of some utterances and a peripheral illocutionary force of others and that those utterances of which it is a central force will either announce themselves as evaluative or contain one of the terms that we normally call evaluative. These suggestions do not require us to hold that every utterance containing an evaluative term will have either a central or a peripheral evaluative force, which is false.

Let us take, for example, the two sentences of the English language 'This is a good sheet' and 'This is a snow-white sheet'. As such they differ only in the substitution of the adjective 'snow-white' for the adjective 'good'. Let us agree, in conformity with the whole argument of this chapter, that either may be used in an utterance which has the illocutionary force of commendation and either may be used in an utterance which has the illocutionary force of description. Now he who assents to 'This is a good sheet' with the force of commendation cannot dissent from 'This is a good sheet' with the force of description, and he who assents to 'This is a good sheet' with the force of description cannot dissent from 'This is a good sheet' with the force of commendation. Thus the forces of description and commendation are both central to this utterance. On the other hand, he who assents to 'This is a snow-white sheet' as a description, with descriptive force, need not assent to it as a commendation, for he may hold eccentric views about the criteria of merit for sheets; but he who assents to 'This is a snow-white sheet' as a commendation cannot dissent from it as a description. Thus in the case of 'This is a snow-white sheet' description is a central and commendation is a peripheral illocutionary force. It seems clear that this difference, that in the one case commendation is a central and the other is a peripheral illocutionary force, can only be explained by the fact that in one case the utterance contains the adjective 'good' and in the other the adjective 'snow-white'. I mark this difference by calling 'good' an evaluative term, but not 'snow-white'. There is no need for us to claim or admit that 'Is this a good red pigment?' will therefore be an utterance with commendatory force.

If, then, 'This is a good sheet' has commendation as a central illocutionary force but 'This is a snow-white sheet' has not, and if the only difference between them is that the one contains the word 'good' and the other the word 'snow-white', it seems reasonable to say that part of understanding the meaning of 'good' is knowing that it differs in this way from 'snow-white'. So the type of theory that we have been considering in this book does help us with the understanding of the meaning of evaluative terms, in spite of its errors. We must not say, as we have so far done, that to say 'This is a good X' is to commend it, nor regard this as a partial account of the meaning of the term 'good', but rather claim that the meaning of 'good' is such that when it fills the blank space in utterances of the form 'This is a ... X' commendation is a central illocutionary force of the utterance.

If our man from Mars were perfecting his knowledge of English by observing how we used words in different contexts he might notice that there were observable differences between apples which we classed as Cox's Orange Pippin and those which we classed as Bramleys; he might notice that there were also observable differences between those that we classed as good and those that we classed as bad. He might become an infallible answerer of such questions as 'Is this a Cox's or a Bramley?' and 'Is this a good or a bad apple?'; but until he had realised that in the one case his answers had commendation as a central illocutionary force and the other had not he would not have realised fully the meanings of the words and thus learnt the difference between botanical classification and grading.

Certainly this account of the meaning of 'good' in terms of a central illocutionary force of commendation is not a full account of it. Judgements of goodness are, as we have already insisted, on the basis of certain standards or criteria of the kind in question or from a selected point of view. It is this aspect, underestimated by the emotivists, that Ziff and Searle have seized on when they offer as accounts of the meaning of 'good' such paraphrases as 'satisfies certain interests' (Ziff and Searle), 'meets the criteria or standards of assessment or evaluation' (Searle) and 'satisfies certain needs' (Searle). There is no need to quarrel with this, except on points of detail, provided that it is offered also as only a partial account. But the question does arise about *which* interests have to be satisfied by a thing if it is to be counted as good, what criteria it must satisfy to be counted as good, why these criteria are criteria or standards of assessment or evaluation rather than criteria of another kind. Thus this partial account has to be supplemented. The interests are the interests such that if the thing in question answers to them we are committed to assent to praise and commendation of it; the criteria are those such that we are willing to be committed to favourable evaluation of things that satisfy them; it is this that makes them criteria of assessment or evaluation and not another kind.

Can we, then, offer a definition of 'good' in the light of the results so far obtained? I certainly could not offer a definition, if by that is meant a revealing substitute formula which could be substituted for 'good' in every context without alteration. But perhaps it is possible to offer a definitional formula, a rule for making substitutions. Let us say that 'good' = 'satisfies a description such that no one can correctly dissent from a favourable evaluation (as of some kind or from some point of view) of an object that satisfies that description'. The application of this formula gives the following specimen results:

'This is a good X' = 'This satisfies a description such that no one can correctly dissent from a favourable evaluation of it as of the kind X.'

'This is good from the Y point of view' = 'This satisfies a description such that no one can correctly dissent from a favourable evaluation of it from the Y point of view'

'If this is good we should buy it' = 'if this satisfies a description

such that no one can correctly dissent from a favourable evaluation
of it, we should buy it'

'Is this good' = 'Does this satisfy etc.'

One possible objection to this formula must be immediately
accepted; it presupposes that 'good' is always used in either the
'of a kind' or the 'from a point of view way'. Such a presupposition
is unjustified and implausible. Our formula is certainly unlikely to
be satisfactory in detail for all uses of 'good'.

But there is another more interesting objection to be faced. In
our previous discussion we had said that anyone who assented to
'This is good' with any other illocutionary force must assent to it
with commendatory force. But it can be objected to my account of
the meaning of 'good' that a person who does not accept the criteria
of merit that I employ might agree that an object satisfied the
description on the basis of which I count it good, but be unwilling
to assent to an assertion that it was good with any illocutionary
force. This is true enough, but it is not really an objection. As has
already been argued in an earlier chapter, our use of 'good' does
presuppose agreement on the proper standards of merit; in other
words, we use the term 'good' as inter-subjectively valid. Therefore
any account of the meaning of 'good' must incorporate this presupposition. I cannot say 'By the erroneous standards that I am
employing, this is good' or 'By my standards this is good, but it
would be equally legitimate to employ other standards according
to which it would be bad'. I can admit that my standards may be
erroneous, but when I use the word 'good' in such utterances as
'This is good', 'If this is good . . .' and 'Is this good?' it is presupposed that they are not erroneous. To say 'My standards of
judging whether this sort of thing is good may be erroneous'
means, according to our definitional formula, 'The descriptive
criteria for this kind of thing such that I regard people who
acknowledge them to be satisfied as unable correctly to dissent
from favourable evaluation may be the wrong ones', which is
perfectly in order; but when I use these criteria I presuppose then
that they are correct. Further our use of 'good' presupposes in

ordinary contexts that others share our standards. It would be deceitful, an abuse of speech, if, knowing that by your standards a thing would be bad which is good by the standards I recognise, I were to say simply and without qualification that it was good. It would be deceitful because you would be entitled to presuppose agreed standards. If I unwittingly employ standards different from yours there is no deceit, but there is a breakdown in communication, for the same reason. We cannot discuss whether a thing is good, engage in standard-using discourse, without this presupposed agreement on standards. If somebody comes along and says 'I don't agree with your way of judging goodness' he is acknowledging that we cannot co-operatively discuss the question of what in fact is good. But he is using the word 'goodness' in accordance with our definitional formula. He is disagreeing with us about which description requires assent to favourable evaluation. Thus in all our use of the term 'good' there is a presupposition that there is some correct set of standards for every kind and from every point of view, and in discussions of whether certain things are good it is presupposed that we all share the correct ones. Whether these presuppositions of the use of 'good' are justified is no doubt a question to which more than one answer may be reasonably supported; the present contention is only that our use of 'good' is such that the question does arise, as it would not if the presuppositions were not made.

But we still have to face the problem of the relation of judgements of goodness, with their central illocutionary force of commendation or some form of favourable evaluation, to utterances of the kind 'I commend this', 'I recommend this' and 'I approve of this'. To say 'This is good' is to make a true or false statement, possibly not with evaluative force, even though that force is central. To say 'I commend this' or 'I recommend this' is to produce a performative which is neither true nor false; it is to perform an act which manifests a favourable attitude. To say 'This is good' with commendatory illocutionary force is not simply to commend though often in saying it one is commending; having said this with that force to add 'I commend it' is not to repeat oneself; but in adding it one is making clear the illocutionary force, not taking a further step. This is what it is to say something with commendatory force. It is perhaps even wrong to say that 'I commend this' has the illocutionary force of commendation. *In* saying something was good I may have been commending it. But it would be more accurate to say that saying 'I commend this' *is* commending it than that *in* saying it one is commending it. Of course, 'Does he commend (recommend, approve of) this' is an utterance raising a question of truth or falsity, and it has a force. But the question raised is not an evaluative one and the force is that of questioning.

In the light of our earlier study of the attitude of approval and the above facts, our ambivalence on the question whether 'approve', 'commend' and the like are to be counted as evaluative terms is intelligible enough. We are inclined to include them because we have to explain ultimately the evaluative character of the term 'good' by reference to them; we have in the end to exclude them because of the serious logical differences between their function and that of terms like 'good'. Maybe we could find some wider tests for evaluative terms which would embrace them; it would not be wrong to attempt to do so. But according to the tests that we adopted they must be excluded, and this need not perplex us.

The conclusion to the whole argument of this chapter must therefore be that we must distinguish carefully, as we had not previously carefully distinguished, the act of commending from a judgement of goodness with the illocutionary force of commendation and the illocutionary force of commendation from the meaning of sentences uttered with that force. But the more extreme conclusion drawn by some that we should cease altogether from referring to such terms as 'good' as terms of commendation or evaluative terms and should regard the illocutionary force of commendation as something which has no bearing at all on the meaning of the term 'good' is not correct. That ascriptions of goodness, unlike the ascription of most characteristics, have a central illocutionary force of favourable evaluation is a fact which is relevant to the meaning of 'good' and which justifies us in referring to it as an evaluative term.

Finally, the relation of this chapter to Chapter 10 requires elucidation. In Chapter 10 we took it that 'better' could be regarded as the paradigm of an evaluative term and offered a test for whether other terms were evaluative; this was that a term V was favourably evaluative if, and only if, it would be an abuse of language to deny that in so far as a thing was V it was better than a non-V thing. A similar test was given for unfavourably evaluative terms. But we have now given an account of what it is that makes 'good' an evaluative term; in brief, 'good' is an evaluative term because its presence in certain utterances gives to them a central favourably evaluative illocutionary force. It is clear that if this account of evaluative terms is correct it renders the test given in chapter X superfluous to the economy of the argument. We could now say that 'charming', for example, was an evaluative term because favourable evaluation was a central illocutionary force of 'This is charming'; the test that what was charming was, *pro tanto*, better than what was not charming has become superfluous.

Lest the reader be perplexed I point out this superfluity now. But the superfluity to the economy of the argument does not necessarily render Chapter 10 otiose or redundant. In the first place it was desirable to offer a test that was independent of my no doubt contentious distinction of central and peripheral illocutionary forces. In the second place it is not without interest that the two tests give the same results; 'charming' will be evaluative on both tests, 'niggers' will be evaluative on neither. This congruence suggests that if one test is sound the other has at least some merit, for it would be surprising if a wholly invalid test led to the same results as a valid one.

12

CONCLUSION

Our examination of the emotive theory of ethics is now, if not complete, at an end. We have seen how the emotivists appealed to a new type of meaning, which they called emotive meaning, both to escape from the sterile epistemological dispute whether 'good' was a natural or a non-natural characteristic, and, still more importantly, in order to explain why ethical discourse committed the speaker and called for more than mere theoretical assent in the hearer.

We have found much to criticise in the account given of emotive meaning. Too much stress was laid on the mere causal properties of, arising from and stimulating emotion, instead of on the forces of expression and (for example) invocation. Still more importantly, the stress laid on emotion, imperfectly distinguished from and indeed confused with attitudes, led to the mistaken view that evaluation was an entirely non-rational element in human behaviour, to which the concepts of truth and falsity, of validity and invalidity, could not be applied. We have corrected this error by insisting that an evaluation commits one to an attitude, and that attitudes are in general but tenuously connected with emotion, since thoughts, words and deeds, are much more central manifestations of them. It is in attitudes so interpreted that we can find disagreement, not in emotion; disagreement is possible because attitudes are adopted and maintained, need to be rationally grounded and can be attacked and defended.

The criticism made on these lines I obviously regard as justified since I have made it. But it is important to see that it is criticism that arises out of the emotivist position, criticism that we are able to make precisely as a result of the formulation of the emotivist position. This is quite a different matter from the mere dismissal of error on grounds which could easily be arrived at without consideration of the error itself.

In Chapter 11 we have had to go further with our criticism. What was presented as a new sort of meaning we have had to recognise as being rather a force of utterance, though we have claimed that a recognition of it is not irrelevant to the clarification of the meaning of evaluative terms. But, however erroneous, the theses of the emotivists were once again basic to the criticism of them subsequently offered. The opening paragraphs of Austin's *How to Do Things with Words*, the work in which the illocutionary force of utterances was first distinguished from meaning, make it clear that he regarded such moves as the emotive theory as the beginning of the recognition of what he called the 'descriptivist fallacy'. Thus even in the criticism of Chapter 11, the most hostile of all, we are using ammunition which we would not have had at our disposal but for the work done by those criticised.

The emotive theory, then, seems to me to be wrong in many ways. But we should see its errors not as false moves to be retracted and quickly forgotten but as the imperfections of the early formulation of insights which have become of great importance to modern philosophy. It is this fact that justifies giving to it the sort of detailed consideration that has been given to it in this book.

SELECT BIBLIOGRAPHY

AYER, A. J. *Language, Truth and Logic* (Gollancz, London, 1936).

BARNES, W. H. F. 'A Suggestion about Value' in *Analysis* (1934).

BRITTEN, K. *Communication* (Routledge and Kegan Paul, London, 1939).

BROAD, C. D. 'Is "goodness" the name of a simple non-natural quality?' in *Proceedings of the Aristotelian Society* (1933–4).

CARNAP, R. *Philosophy and Logical Syntax* (Psyche Miniatures, London, 1935).

EDWARDS, P. *The Logic of Moral Discourse* (Free press Glencoe, III, 1955).

KERNER, G. C. *The Revolution in Ethical Theory* (Clarendon Press, Oxford, 1966).

MACDONALD, M. 'Ethics and the Ceremonial Use of Language' in *Philosophical Analysis* Ed. Black M. (Cornell U.P., Ithica N.Y., 1950).

MOORE, G. E. *Philosophical Studies* (Routledge and Kegan Paul, London, 1922).

OGDEN, C. K. and RICHARDS I. A. *The Meaning of Meaning* (Routledge and Kegan Paul, London, 1923).

PITCHER, G. 'On Approval' in *Philosophical Review* (1958).

ROBINSON, R. 'The Emotive Theory of Ethics' in *Proceedings of the Aristotelian Society Supplementary Volume* (1948).

SEARLE, J. R. 'Meaning and Speech-Acts' in *Metaphysics and Experience* Ed. Rollins, C. D. (Univ. of Pittsburgh Press, 1962).

STEBBING, S. *A Modern Introduction to Logic* (Methuen, London, 1930).

STEVENSON, C. L. 'The Emotive Meaning of Ethical Terms' in *Mind* (1937).
'Persuasive Definitions' in *Mind* (1938).
Ethics and Language (Yale U.P., New Haven, 1944).
Facts and Values (Yale U.P., New Haven, 1963).
'Ethical Fallibility' in *Ethics and Society* Ed. De George (Doubleday Anchor, Garden City, N.Y.).

ZIFF, P. *Semantic Analysis* (Cornell U.P., Ithica, N.Y., 1960).

INDEX